Practice Papers for SQA Exams

Intermediate 1 | Units 1, 2 and 3

Mathematics

Introduction	3
Practice Exam Paper A	7
Practice Exam Paper B	19
Practice Exam Paper C	29
Practice Exam Paper D	39
Worked Answers	51

Text © 2010 Dominic Ferla
Design and layout © 2010 Leckie & Leckie
01/150110

All rights reserved. No part of this publication may be reproduced, stored in a retrieval system, or transmitted in any form or by any means, electronic, mechanical, photocopying, recording or otherwise, without prior permission in writing from Leckie & Leckie Ltd. Legal action will be taken by Leckie & Leckie Ltd against any infringement of our copyright.

The right of Dominic Ferla to be identified as author of this Work has been asserted by him in accordance with sections 77 and 78 of the Copyright, Designs and Patents Act 1988.

ISBN 978-1-84372-799-6

Published by
Leckie & Leckie Ltd, 4 Queen Street, Edinburgh, EH2 1JE
Tel: 0131 220 6831 Fax: 0131 225 9987
enquiries@leckieandleckie.co.uk   www.leckieandleckie.co.uk

A CIP Catalogue record for this book is available from the British Library.

Leckie & Leckie Ltd is a division of Huveaux plc.

Questions and answers in this book do not emanate from SQA. All of our entirely new and original Practice Papers have been written by experienced authors working directly for the publisher.

Introduction

Layout of the Book

This book contains practice exam papers, which mirror the actual SQA exam as much as possible. The layout, paper colour and question level are all similar to the actual exam that you will sit, so that you are familiar with what the exam paper will look like.

The answer section is at the back of the book. Each answer contains a worked out answer or solution so that you can see how the right answer has been arrived at. The answers also include practical tips on how to tackle certain types of questions, details of how marks are awarded and advice on just what the examiners will be looking for.

Revision advice is provided in this introductory section of the book, so please read on!

How to use This Book

The Practice Papers can be used in two main ways:

1. You can complete an entire practice paper as preparation for the final exam. If you would like to use the book in this way, you can either complete the practice paper under exam style conditions by setting yourself a time for each paper and answering it as well as possible without using any references or notes. Alternatively, you can answer the practice paper questions as a revision exercise, using your notes to produce a model answer. Your teacher may mark these for you.

2. You can use the Topic Index at the front of this book to find all the questions within the book that deal with a specific topic. This allows you to focus specifically on areas that you particularly want to revise or, if you are mid-way through your course, it lets you practise answering exam-style questions for just those topics that you have studied.

Revision Advice

Work out a revision timetable for each week's work in advance – remember to cover all of your subjects and to leave time for homework and breaks. For example:

Day	6pm–6.45pm	7pm–8pm	8.15pm–9pm	9.15pm–10pm
Monday	Homework	Homework	English Revision	Chemistry Revision
Tuesday	Maths Revision	Physics Revision	Homework	Free
Wednesday	Geography Revision	Modern Studies Revision	English Revision	French Revision
Thursday	Homework	Maths Revision	Chemistry Revision	Free
Friday	Geography Revision	French Revision	Free	Free
Saturday	Free	Free	Free	Free
Sunday	Modern Studies Revision	Maths Revision	Modern Studies Revision	Homework

Make sure that you have at least one evening free a week to relax, socialise and re-charge your batteries. It also gives your brain a chance to process the information that you have been feeding it all week.

Arrange your study time into one hour or 30 minutes sessions, with a break between sessions e.g. 6pm–7pm, 7.15pm–7.45pm, 8pm–9pm. Try to start studying as early as possible in the evening when your brain is still alert and be aware that the longer you put off starting, the harder it will be to start!

Study a different subject in each session, except for the day before an exam.

Do something different during your breaks between study sessions – have a cup of tea, or listen to some music. Don't let your 15 minutes expanded into 20 or 25 minutes though!

Have your class notes and any textbooks available for your revision to hand as well as plenty of blank paper, a pen, etc. Revising for a maths exam is often most effective if you try to solve maths problems.

You may like to make a list of 'Key Questions' with the dates of your various attempts (successful or not!). These should be questions that you have struggled with.

Key Question	1st Attempt		2nd Attempt		3rd Attempt	
Textbook P43, Q6b	7/2/10	X	10/2/10	√	17/2/10	√
Practice Exam B Paper 1 Q4	17/2/10	X	20/2/10	X	23/2/10	√
Practice Exam D Paper 2 Q7	2/3/10	X	5/3/10	X		

The method for working this list is as follows:

1. Any attempt at a question should be dated.
2. A tick or cross should be entered to mark the success or failure of each attempt.
3. A date for your next attempt at that question should be entered:

    For an unsuccessful attempt – 3 days later

    For a successful attempt – 1 week later

4. After two successful attempts remove that question from the list as you can assume that the question has been learnt!

Using this 'list' method for revising for your maths exam ensures that your revision is focused on the difficulties you have had and that you are actively trying to overcome these difficulties.

Finally forget or ignore all or some of the advice in this section if you are happy with your present way of studying. Everyone revises differently, so find a way that works for you!

Transfer Your Knowledge

As well as using your class notes and textbooks to revise, these practice papers will also be a useful revision tool as they will help you to get used to answering exam style questions. You may find as you work through the questions that they refer to a case study or an example that you haven't come across before. Don't worry! You may have come across a question or a topic that you have not yet covered in class – check with your teacher. Or it may be the case that the wording or the context of the question is unfamiliar. This is often the case with reasoning questions in the maths exam. Once you examine the worked solutions, in most cases you will find that the question is asking you to apply mathematical techniques with which you are familiar. In either case, you should revisit that question at a later date to check that you can successfully solve it.

Trigger Words

In the practice papers and in the exam itself, a number of 'trigger' words will be used in the questions. These trigger words should help you to identify a process or technique that is expected in your solution to that part of the question. If you familiarise yourself with these trigger words, it will help you to structure your solutions more effectively.

Trigger Word	Meaning/Explanation
Evaluate	Carry out a calculation to give an answer that is a value.
Hence	You must use the result of the previous part of the question to complete your solution. No marks will be awarded if you use an alternative method that does not use the previous answer.
Simplify	This means different things in different contexts: **Surds:** reduce the number under the root sign to the smallest possible by removing square factors. **Fractions:** one fraction, cancelled down, is expected. **Algebraic expressions:** get rid of brackets and gather all like terms together.
Give your answer to…	This is an instruction for the accuracy of your final answer. These instructions must be followed or you will lose a mark.
Algebraically	The method you use must involve algebra e.g. you must solve an equation or simplify an algebraic equation. It is usually stated to avoid trial-and-improvement methods or reading answers from your calculator.
Justify your answer	This is a request for you to indicate clearly your reasoning. Will the examiner know how you reached your solution?
Show all your working	Marks will be allocated for the individual steps in your working. Steps missed out may lose you marks.

In the Exam

Watch your time and pace yourself carefully. Work out roughly how much time you can spend on each answer and try to stick to this.

Be clear before the exam what the instructions are likely to be e.g. how many questions you should answer in each section. The practice papers will help you to become familiar with the exam's instructions.

Read the question thoroughly before you begin to answer it – make sure you know exactly what the question is asking you to do. If the question is in sections e.g. 15a, 15b, 15c, etc, then it is often the case that answers obtained in the earlier sections are used in the later sections of that question.

When you have reached your solution, check it over again. Is your reasoning clear? Will the examiner understand how you arrived at your answer? If in doubt, fill in more details.

If you change your mind, or think that your solution is wrong, don't score it out unless you have another solution to replace it with. Solutions that are not correct can often gain some of the marks available. Do not miss the working out as showing step-by-step working will help you to gain marks even if there is a mistake in the working.

Good luck!

Topic Index

Unit 1	A Paper 1	A Paper 2	B Paper 1	B Paper 2	C Paper 1	C Paper 2	D Paper 1	D Paper 2
Basic Calculations	1	2, 9	1	6	1	4, 8	1	9
Basic Geometry Formulae	10	1, 8, 12	9, 10	1, 8, 12	8	1, 12, 13	10	2, 11, 12
Calculations in Context	5, 8	10	2, 7	2, 11	3	7, 9	2, 3, 6	5
Unit 2								
Graphs, Charts and Tables	2, 3, 4	3, 11	3, 6	7, 10	2, 5, 7	11	4, 9	3, 7
Time, Distance and Speed		5		4	6	5	7	10
The Theorem of Pythagoras		6	4	3	11	2		1
Unit 3								
Basic Algebra	7	4, 7	5	5, 9	9	3, 6	5	4, 8
Graphical Relationships	9	13	8	13	10	10	11	6
Basic Trigonometry Standard Form	6		11		4		8	

Practice Exam A

Mathematics | Intermediate 1 | Units 1, 2 and 3

Practice Papers
For SQA Exams

Exam A
Intermediate 1
Units 1, 2 and 3
Paper 1
Non-calculator

You are allowed 35 minutes to complete this paper.

Do **not** use a calculator.

Try to answer all of the questions in the time allowed, including all of your working.

Full marks will only be awarded where your answer includes any relevant working.

Practice Paper A: Intermediate 1 Mathematics Units 1, 2 and 3

Marks

1. Work out the answers to the following.

   (a) $6 \times (5 - 3) + 7$ 1

   (b) 18×3000 1

   (c) $5 \cdot 82 \div 3$ 1

   (d) 20% of £60   1

2. Jay is taking the sleeper train from Central Station. It departs from Glasgow at 11.45 pm and should arrive in Birmingham by 5.35 am. How long will his journey take?   1

3. Graham wants to buy some accessories for his new games console.
   He passes an advert in a shop window.

   Craig's Consoles

Control Pad	Steering Wheel	Pro Player
£14	£14·50	£15
Eye-Cam	Remote Control	Memory Card
£13·50	£12	£9·50

   Graham wants to
   - buy **four** different accessories
   - one of these must be the game **Pro Player**.
   - spend at most £55.

Page 10

Practice Paper A: Intermediate 1 Mathematics Units 1, 2 and 3

The table below shows **two** possible ways that Graham can do this.

Control Pad		£14·00							
Eye-Cam	£13·50	£13·50							
Steering Wheel	£14·50								
Remote Control	£12·00	£12·00							
Pro Player	£15·00	£15·00							
Memory Card									
Total	£55·00	£54·50							

Complete the above table to show all the ways that Graham can do this.   3

4. The frequency table below shows the number of goals scored per game by a premier league football team over the course of a season.

Number of goals	Frequency	Number of goals × frequency
0	3	0
1	8	8
2	14	28
3	9	
4	1	
5	1	
	Total = 36	Total =

(a) Complete the table above and find the mean number of goals.   3

(b) Write down the modal number of goals.   1

5. A furniture store is holding a closing down sale. A sofa can be bought on hire purchase for a price of £635. There must be a deposit of £85 followed by 11 equal monthly payments. How much will the monthly repayments be?   3

6. On July 13, 1985, the multi-venue rock music concert Live Aid raised $283 600 000 to raise funds for famine relief in Ethiopia. Write this number in Scientific Notation.   2

7. Solve algebraically

$2x + 36 = 9x + 15$ 3

Page 11

8. (a) A group of pupils go on a school trip to Paris.
Each brings with them £80 spending money.
The exchange rate at the time is 1·2 euros to the pound.
How many euros does each pupil receive?

(b) Upon his return, one pupil exchanged the €44 he has left back into pounds sterling.
He received £40.
He was convinced the exchange rate had changed while he had been in Paris.
Is he correct?
Working must be shown.

9. (a) Complete the table for $y = 5 - x$.

x	−3	1	4
y			

(b) Draw the line $y = 5 - x$ on the diagram below.

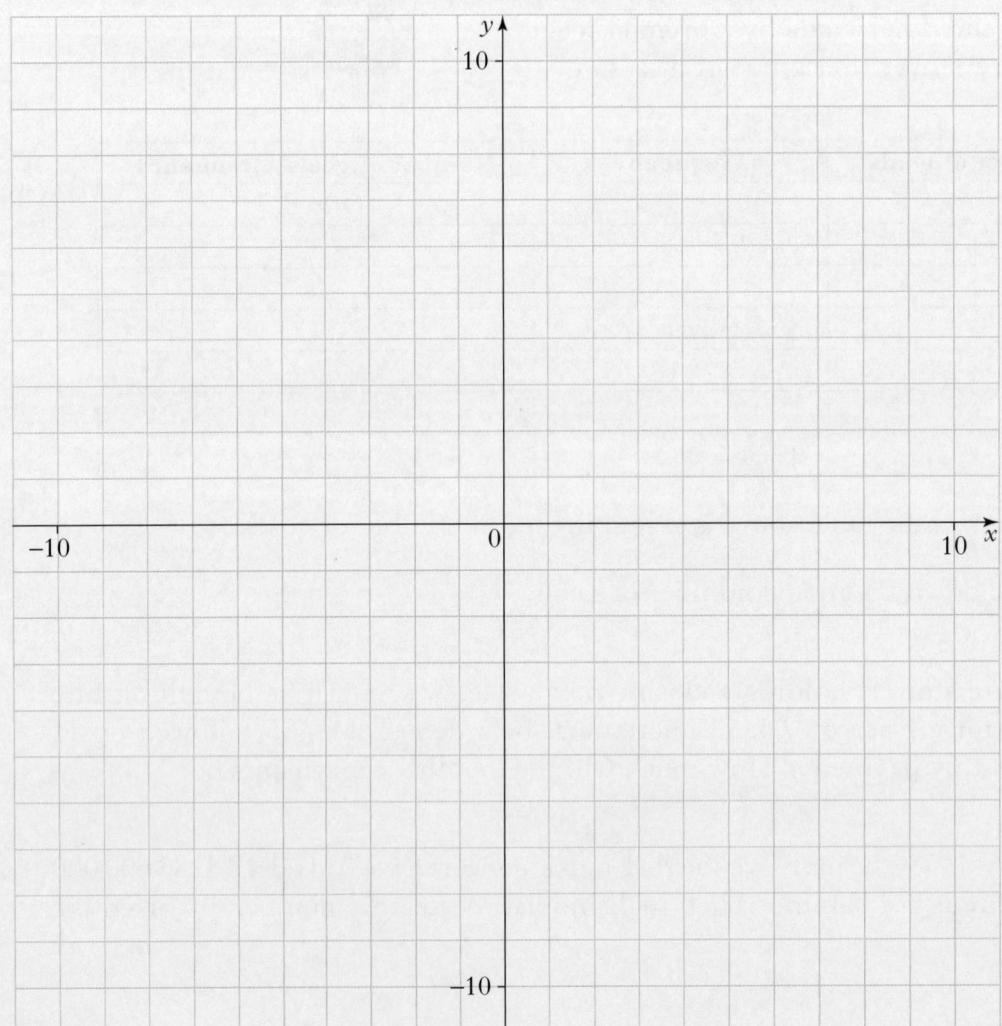

10. Given $a = 2$, $b = 6$ and $c = -4$, find the value of $\dfrac{12a^2}{bc}$.

[End of Question Paper]

Mathematics | Intermediate 1 | Units 1, 2 and 3

Practice Papers
For SQA Exams

**Exam A
Intermediate 1
Units 1, 2 and 3
Paper 2**

You are allowed 55 minutes to complete this paper.

A calculator can be used.

Try to answer all of the questions in the time allowed, including all of your working.

Full marks will only be awarded where your answer includes any relevant working.

Scotland's leading educational publishers

1. (a) Plot the points A(−1, 5), B(−6, 0) and C(−1, −5) on the coordinate diagram below.

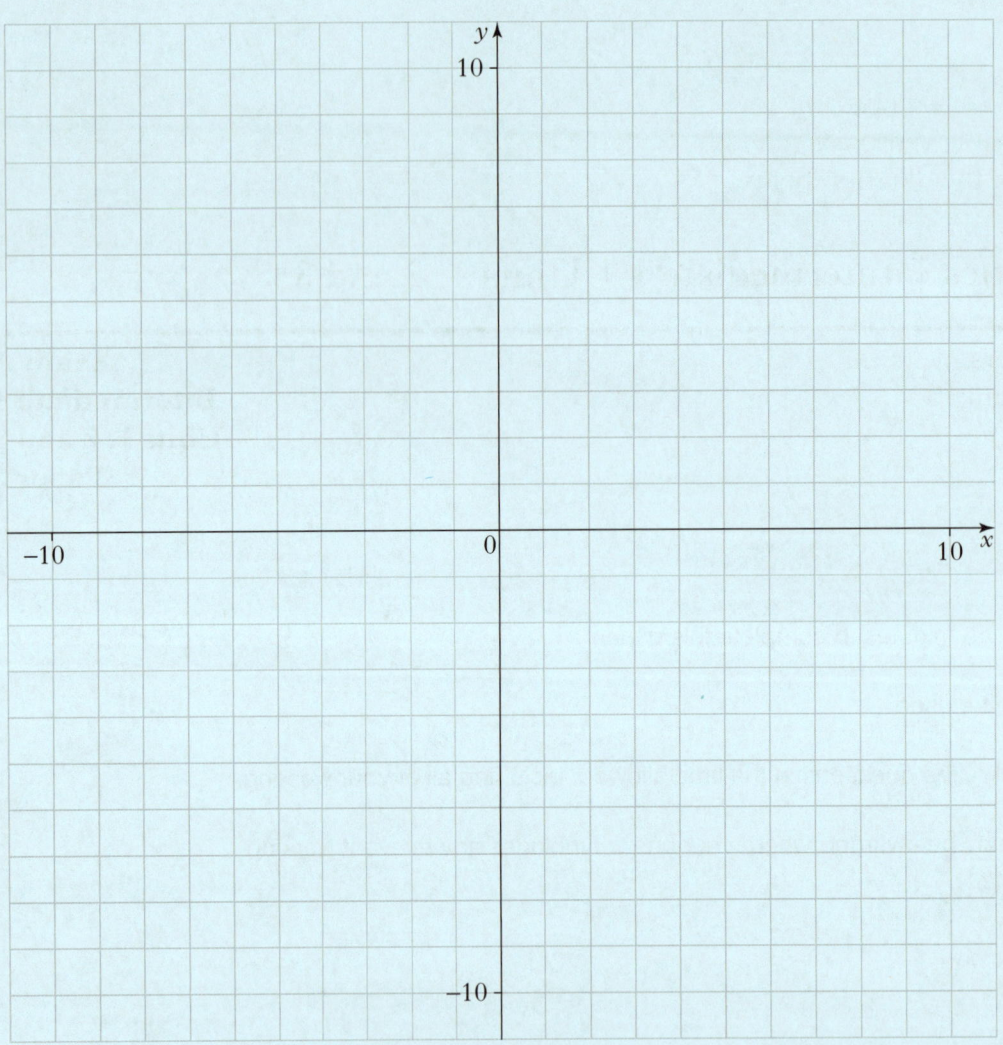

(b) Plot a fourth point D so that ABCD makes a square.

2. During pre-season training, a coach counts the number of left-footers in his 30 man squad. Six of them are found to be left-footed. What percentage of players in his squad are right-footed?

3. Silverstone is the circuit for the British Grand Prix. It has a lap length of 5 km with a Grand Prix consisting of 60 laps. A driver's race time was 2½ hours. What was his average speed, in **kilometres per hour**?

4. Solve algebraically the inequality:

$$3x - 2 > 10$$

Marks

2

5. A gondola can be taken from a pick-up point onto Aonach Mor, the eighth highest mountain in Britain.
The gondola can reach a height of 650m and has a steel cable 700m in length as shown in the diagram below.
Calculate the horizontal distance, x m, between the pick-up point and the base of the mountain.

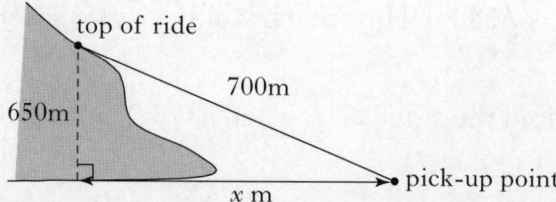

3

6. Cheryl is renewing her car insurance.
A price comparison website listed the following as their 10 cheapest quotations in pounds (£):

120, 160, 180, 210, 230, 260, 300, 340, 360, 400

Calculate

(a) The median

2

(b) The range

2

(c) Cheryl wasn't happy with the results and tried another similar website. This time, the cheapest quotations had a median of £200 and a range of 350. Make **two** valid comparisons between the websites.

2

7. (a) Multiply out the following brackets and simplify:

$$10 + 5(3x + 8)$$

2

(b) Factorise fully:

$$35x - 10$$

2

8. Eric orders a pizza from Roberto's Pizzas.

Calculate the volume of this pizza box, giving your answer in appropriate units. 3

9. The cost of six calculators is £58·80. How much will it cost for seven calculators? 3

10. Using the formula below, find the value of P when $q = 3\cdot2$ and $r = 8$.

$$P = 2r^2 - 25q$$

3

11. A group of friends compared their results in recent French and German exams. Their results are shown in the scattergraph below.

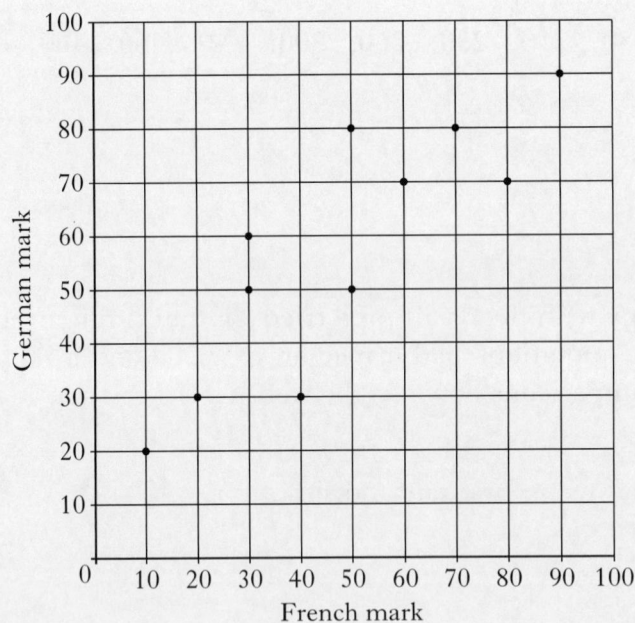

(a) On this scattergraph, draw a line of best fit. 1

(b) Audrey scored 30 in the French exam. Use your line of best fit to estimate her score in the German exam. 1

12. The Mona Lisa the world's most famous painting.
    The painting is fitted with an oak frame with a height of 89cm and a width of 65cm. There is a 6cm gap between the outside of the frame and the painting itself as shown in the diagram below.
    Calculate the area of the wooden frame.

    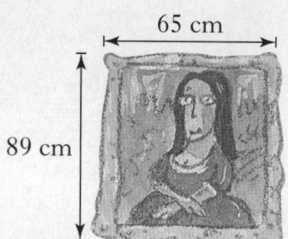

    4

13. A public library provides a wheel-chair ramp for its customers. The British Standards Institution states that a continuous suitable handrail must be provided when a ramp rises more than 20 cm over a 2 metre distance. The library builds the following ramp in front of its main entrance. Will this ramp require a handrail? **Give a reason for your answer**.

    5

    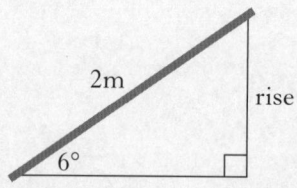

    [End of Question Paper]

Practice Exam B

Mathematics | Intermediate 1 | Units 1, 2 and 3

Practice Papers
For SQA Exams

Exam B
Intermediate 1
Units 1, 2 and 3
Paper 1
Non-calculator

You are allowed 35 minutes to complete this paper.

Do **not** use a calculator.

Try to answer all of the questions in the time allowed, including all of your working.

Full marks will only be awarded where your answer includes any relevant working.

Practice Paper B: Intermediate 1 Mathematics Units 1, 2 and 3

Marks

1. Work out the answers to the following.

   (a) 8·46 − 3·8   1

   (b) $66\frac{2}{3}\%$ of £2700   1

   (c) 5·6 × 400   1

2. An interpreter uses this rule to work out her charge in pounds (£) for translating paragraphs of French text into English.

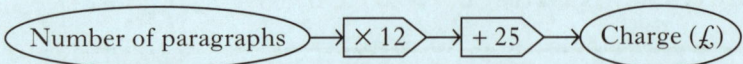

   How much would she charge for translating six paragraphs of text?   2

3. A football match was televised recently. There was 90 minutes of normal playing time. The interval lasted 15 minutes. Extra-time was played and lasted 30 minutes. After that the game was decided on penalties.
   The match kicked-off at 7·45 pm.
   What time did the penalty shoot-out start?   2

4. There are 30 raffle tickets in a hat. Three tickets win a cuddly toy, one ticket wins £10 and the rest are losing tickets. What is the probability that you will win:

   (a) £10?   1

   (b) a cuddly toy?   2

5. Solve the following equation

   $6x + 24 = 10x - 4$ 3

6. The number of runs scored in cricket during a recent test match is shown in the frequency table below.

Number of runs	Frequency	Number of runs × frequency
4	6	24
5	15	75
6	10	
7	7	
8	2	
	Total = 40	Total =

Page 22

(a) By completing the table above, calculate the mean number of runs per cricketer.

(b) Write down the modal number of runs.

7. A taxi driver will charge £3·00 for the hire of the taxi and a further £1·20 per mile. Mary catches a taxi to go down town which is a journey of 7 miles. What will she be charged?

8. (a) Complete the table for $y = 4 - 2x$.

x	−4	0	2
y			

(b) Using the table above, draw the line $y = 4 - 2x$ on the grid.

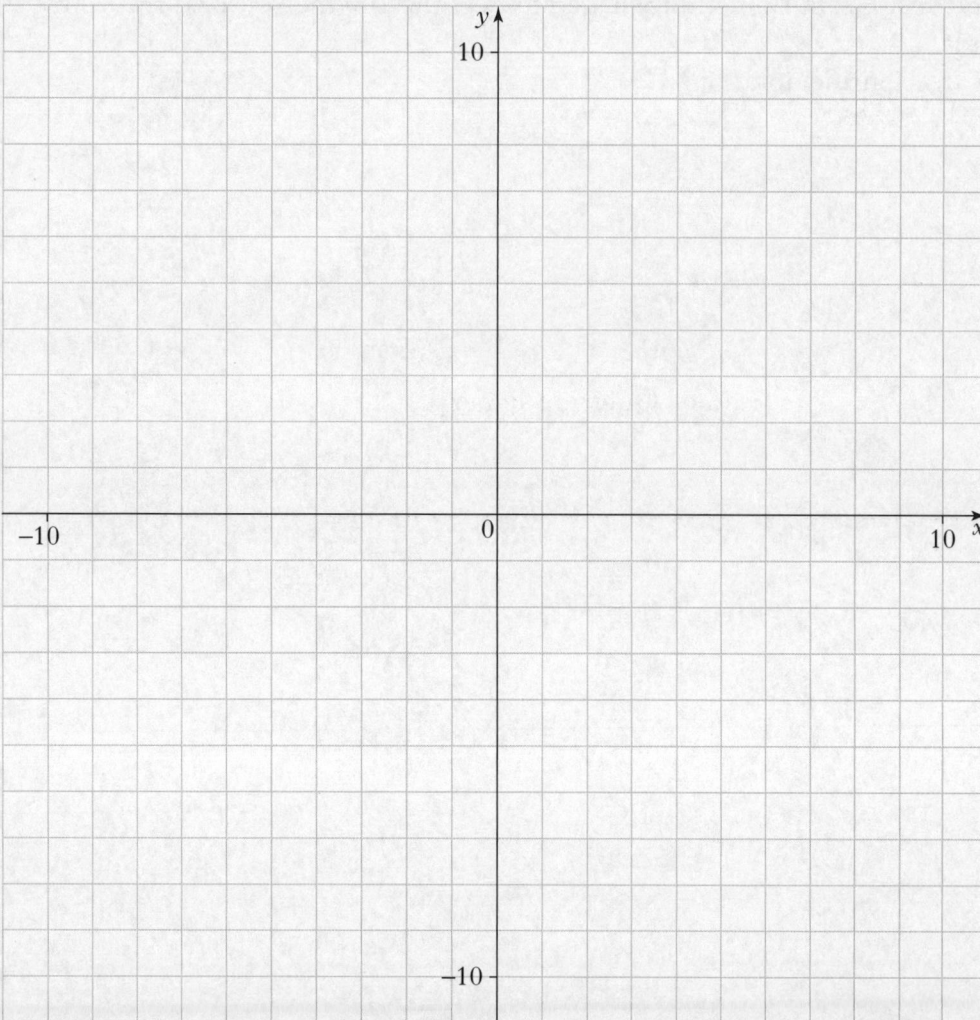

Marks

3

1

2

2

2

9. Evaluate $\dfrac{3ab}{c}$ when $a = -2$, $b = -5$ and $c = 9$.

10. Amy received £160 for her sixteenth birthday.

She sets up a savings account.
The bank offer her interest at the rate of 5% per annum.
How much should be in her account after 9 months?

11. During the 2008 Olympics, despite attempting to tie his shoelace before crossing the line, Usain Bolt still managed to beat the 100 metre world record by 0·15 seconds.
Write 0·15 in scientific notation.

[End of Question Paper]

Mathematics | Intermediate 1 | Units 1, 2 and 3

Practice Papers
For SQA Exams

Exam B
Intermediate 1
Units 1, 2 and 3
Paper 2

You are allowed 55 minutes to complete this paper.

A calculator can be used.

Try to answer all of the questions in the time allowed, including all of your working.

Full marks will only be awarded where your answer includes any relevant working.

1. Calculate the volume of the cube below, rounding your answer to the nearest **thousand**.

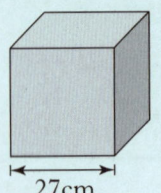

27cm

2

2. Upon returning from Oslo, George changed 468 Norwegian Kroner into pounds (£).
How many pounds (£) did George get?
The exchange rate at the time was £1 = 10·40 kroner.

2

3. Julie is buying a television for her new house. She checks the prices of the tv in the top five electrical stores on her local high street.

£830, £750, £780, £940, £690

Calculate:

(a) The median.

2

(b) The range.

2

A new shopping centre has just opened on the outskirts of town. Julie conducts the same check there and finds that the median price of a television is £810 and the range is 300.

(c) Make **two** valid comparisons between the price of televisions in the high street and the prices in the shopping centre.

2

4. A tent at a campsite is in the shape of an isosceles triangle.

4 m

6 m

It has a width of 6m and a sloping side of length 4m as shown in the diagram.

Calculate the height of the tent.

4

5. Solve the following inequality.

$7x + 4 < 32$

2

Page 26

6. Scott has 150 CDs in his collection.
He finds that 90 of them belong to the genre 'Heavy Metal'.
What percentage of his CDs are of the 'Heavy Metal' genre?   3

7. A train leaves Glasgow Central at 9·50 am.
It travels the 150 miles to Aberdeen at an average speed of 60 miles per hour.

(a) How long did the journey take?   3

(b) At what time did the train arrive in Aberdeen?   1

8. A 10 p coin has a radius of 14mm.

Calculate the circumference of the coin, giving your answer in centimetres.   4

9. (a) Expand the brackets and simplify:

$7 + 5(8x - 2)$ 2

(b) Factorise:

$18x + 36$ 2

10. A garage failed 180 cars in their MOT. It lists the four most common faults that failed the cars. The results are shown in the pie chart below:

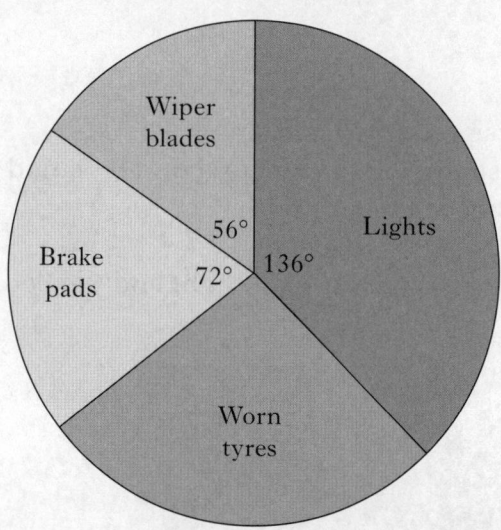

How many of the cars failed due to worn tyres?   3

11. A point has coordinates (x, y). Its distance from the origin can be calculated using the formula $d = \sqrt{x^2 + y^2}$.

Use the formula to find how far the point (7, 24) is from the origin.

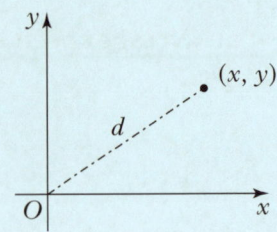

3

12. A bathroom mirror consists of a rectangle with a semicircular piece of glass in the centre as shown.
Calculate the area of the mirror.

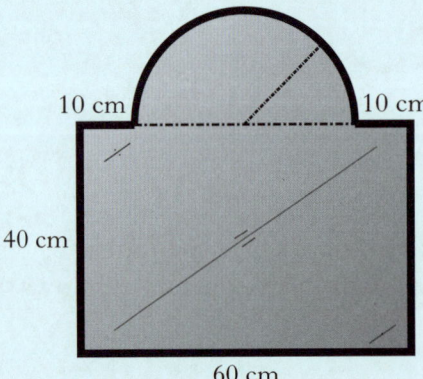

6

13. A café has an open-mike session every Tuesday.
The performers are lit by a spotlight attached to the wall behind them.
The spotlight is 2·5 metres above the ground.
It produces a beam of light 5 metres in length.
Calculate the size of the angle between the spotlight and the floor.

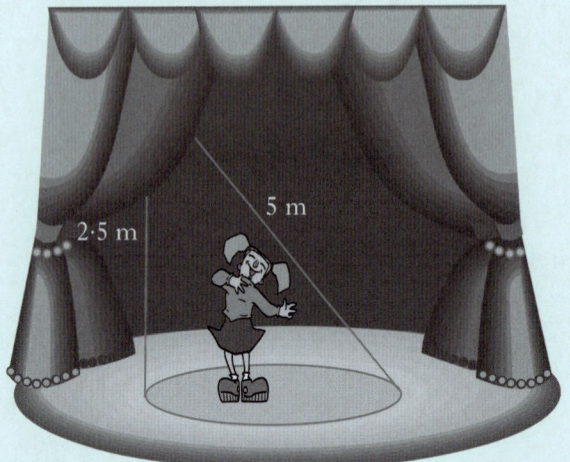

4

[End of Question Paper]

Practice Exam C

Mathematics | Intermediate 1 | Units 1, 2 and 3

Practice Papers
For SQA Exams

**Exam C
Intermediate 1
Units 1, 2 and 3
Paper 1
Non-calculator**

You are allowed 35 minutes to complete this paper.

Do **not** use a calculator.

Try to answer all of the questions in the time allowed, including all of your working.

Full marks will only be awarded where your answer includes any relevant working.

Practice Paper C: Intermediate 1 Mathematics Units 1, 2 and 3

Marks

1. (a) Find 9·62 − 3·983

    (b) Find 5% of £70

    (c) Find $\frac{5}{9}$ of 135

1

2

2

2. The flight from Glasgow to Malaga takes 3 hrs 20 minutes.
   A plane departs from Glasgow at 07·10.
   Malaga clocks are 1 hour ahead of those in Scotland.
   What will the clock in Malaga read when the Glasgow flight arrives?

2

3. A two bedroom flat was purchased for £80 000.
   Building insurance is compulsory when buying a property.
   An insurance firm charges an annual premium of £2·50 per £1000 insured.
   How much would it cost to insure this flat for a year?

2

4. Ben Nevis is the highest mountain in the British Isles.
   Its summit stands at 1 344 000 millimetres above sea-level.
   Write this number in scientific notation.

2

5. Stewart has moved in to an unfurnished flat. He wants to buy some furniture for the living room and sees an advert in a local newspaper:

Stewart wants to
- buy **four** different items of furniture
- one of the four items should be a **Coffee Table**.
- spend a **maximum** of £100.

The table below shows **two** possible combination of **four** items of furniture that Stewart can buy.

Page 32

Coffee Table	£25	£25				
Side Table	£15	£15				
Shelving Unit	£40	£40				
Set of Cushions		£10				
Rug	£20					
Lamp						
Total	£100	£90				

Complete the above table to show all combinations of furniture that Stewart can afford to buy.   **3**

6. Work out the answers to the following.

(a) $3 \times (-3) \times 3$ **1**

(b) $12 - (-8)$ **1**

7. The number of coins given in change in a local supermarket one morning is recorded in the following frequency table.

Number of coins	Frequency
1	9
2	12
3	18
4	4
5	5
6	2
	Total = 50

Using the table above, calculate the mean number of coins received in change per customer.   **4**

8. Find the value of $3x^2 - 2y$ when $x = -2$ and $y = 3$.

9. Solve the following inequality:

$$7x - 3 > 39$$

10. (a) Complete the table for $y = 2 - 4x$.

x	-2	-1	0	1
y		6		

(b) Using the above table, draw the line $y = 2 - 4x$ on the grid.

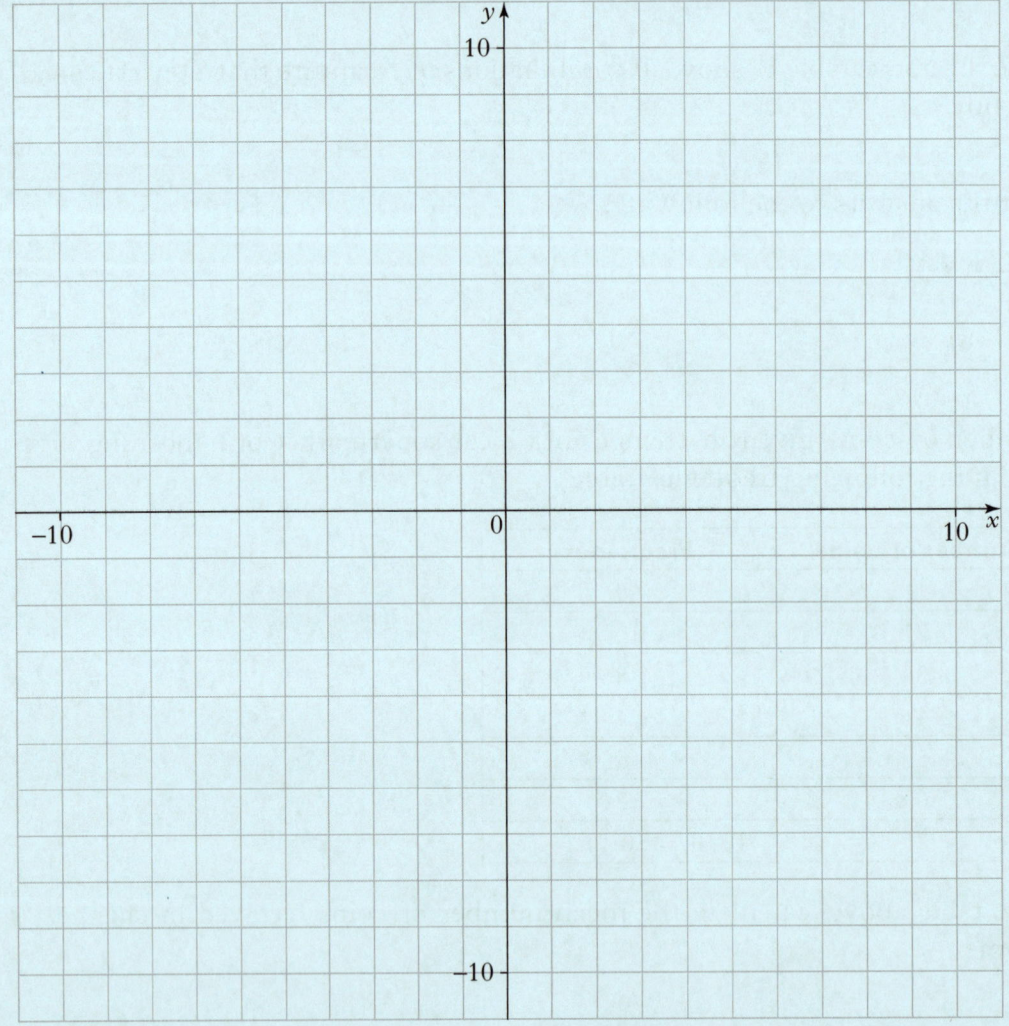

11. In the Costa Del Sol it is said to be sunny 300 days a year. A date is picked at random in the year 2011. What is the probability that it will not be a sunny day.

[End of Question Paper]

Mathematics | Intermediate 1 | Units 1, 2 and 3

Practice Papers
For SQA Exams

Exam C
Intermediate 1
Units 1, 2 and 3
Paper 2

You are allowed 55 minutes to complete this paper.

A calculator can be used.

Try to answer all of the questions in the time allowed, including all of your working.

Full marks will only be awarded where your answer includes any relevant working.

Practice Paper C: Intermediate 1 Mathematics Units 1, 2 and 3

Marks

1. (a) Plot the points P(−5, −2), Q(1, 4) and R(−2, −5) on the coordinate diagram below:-

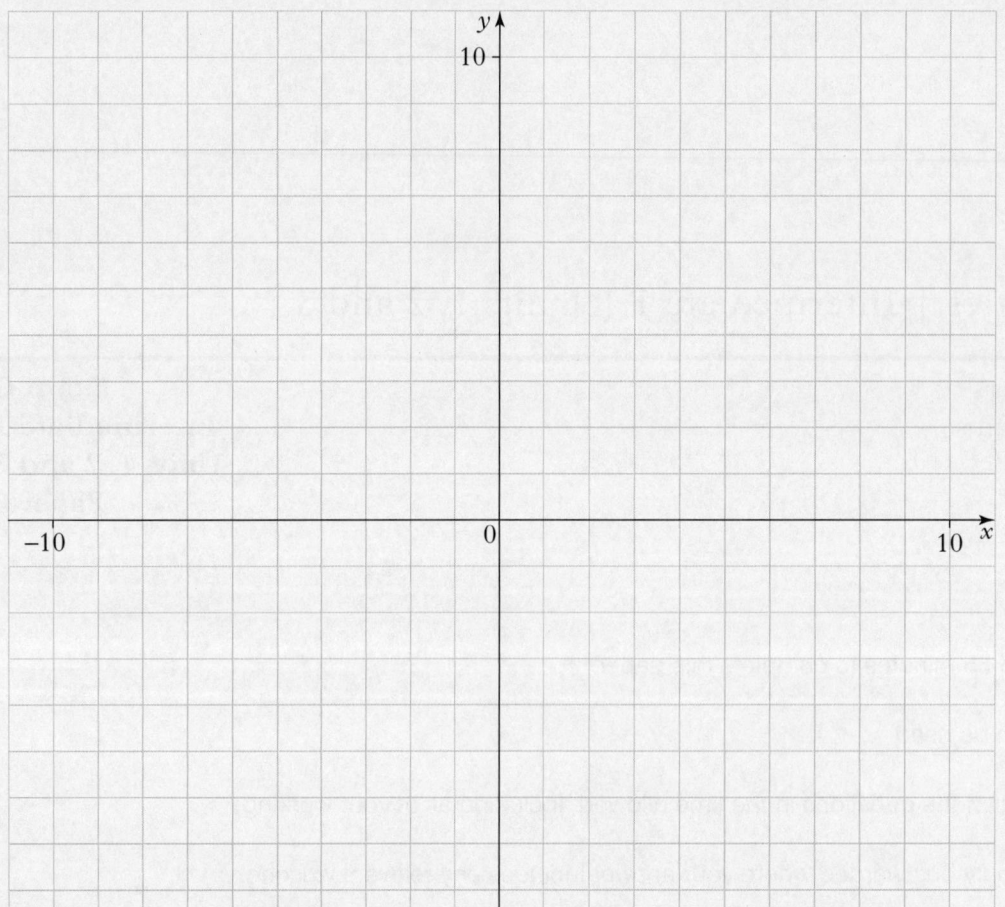

(b) PQRS is a rectangle. Find the coordinates of S.

2. At an airport check-in, a customer must pay extra if their suitcase weighs over 20 kilograms. The weights of ten different suitcases were recorded below:

18, 15, 23, 20, 19, 18, 24, 10, 12, 14

Calculate:

(a) The mean weight of the sample.

(b) The median weight of the sample.

3. (a) Multiply out the brackets and simplify:

$$4(3x - 2) - 5x$$

(b) Factorise fully:

$$16 - 12x$$

2

1

2

2

2

2

Practice Paper C: Intermediate 1 Mathematics Units 1, 2 and 3

Marks

4. Claire decides to open a savings account for her grandchildren. She deposits the sum of £3500. The bank gives her an interest rate of 3% per annum. How much interest will be earned after four months?

3

5. Dominic has locked himself out of his second floor flat.
   He decides to use a ladder to climb in the open window.
   He places the ladder 5m away from the wall and his flat is 12m above the ground.
   Calculate the length of the ladder.

3

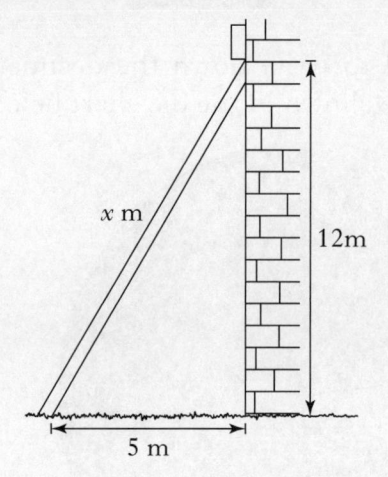

x m

12m

5 m

6. Solve algebraically:

   $$13x - 2 = 6x + 19$$

3

7. Daniel travelled from Canada to London for a business meeting.
   He changed 2160 Canadian dollars into pounds (£).
   He had to spend £800 in London before travelling to another meeting in Monte Carlo, where he changed what was left into euros.
   How many euros did Daniel have to spend in Monte Carlo?
   £1 = 1·80 dollars
   £1 = 1·17 euros

3

8. Marie bought an extra ticket for a music festival for £200. She resold it on the internet for £225. Calculate her profit, giving your answer as a percentage of the purchase price.

3

9. Use the formula below to find the value of A when $b = 4\cdot3$ and $c = 11\cdot7$.

   $$A = \sqrt{b+c}$$

3

10. On a salvage mission, a submarine descends below sea-level at an angle of 35°. At what depth is the submarine after traveling 250 metres horizontally?

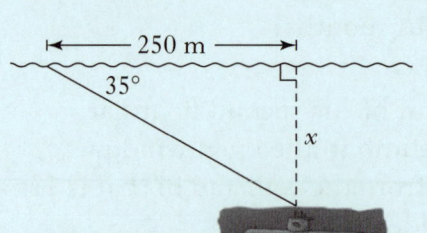

11. A registration class were asked to write down the destination of their recent summer holiday. The results are shown in the pie chart below.

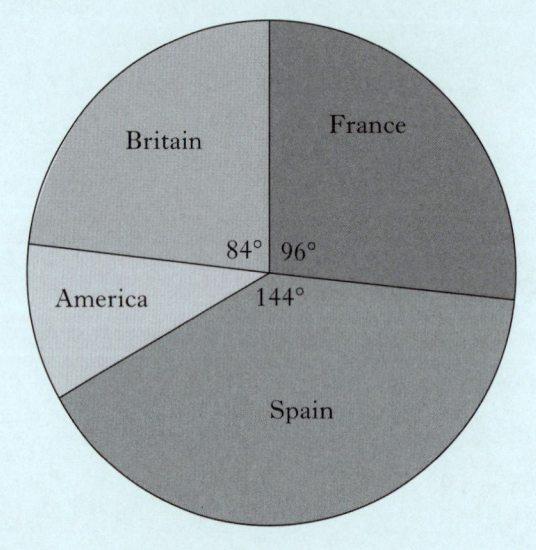

Of the 30 pupils in the class, how many went to America?

12. The volume of this rubix cube is 216 cm³.
What is its length?

13. Pizza Hoose sells its ham and mixed peppers pizza on two different bases:
    The Deep Pan   The Big Feast
    (8 equal slices)   (6 equal slices)

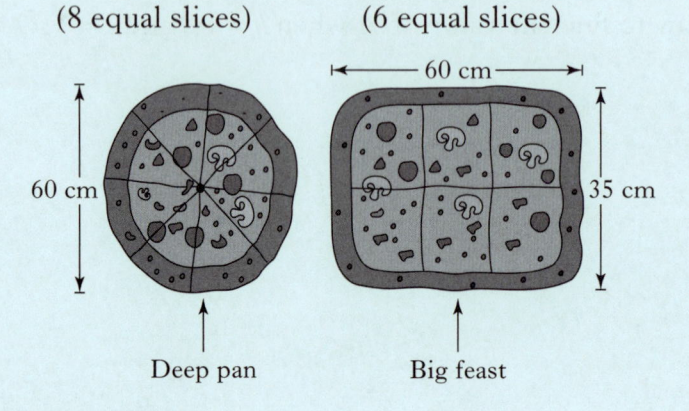

Which slice of pizza has the greater area?

[End of Question Paper]

Marks
4

3

3

5

Practice Exam D

Mathematics | Intermediate 1 | Units 1, 2 and 3

Practice Papers
For SQA Exams

**Exam D
Intermediate 1
Units 1, 2 and 3
Paper 1
Non-calculator**

You are allowed 35 minutes to complete this paper.

Do **not** use a calculator.

Try to answer all of the questions in the time allowed, including all of your working.

Full marks will only be awarded where your answer includes any relevant working.

	Marks

1. Work out the answers to the following.

(a) $9 + 16·37 - 4·8$ — 2

(b) $0·39 \times 40$ — 1

2. An LCD television can be bought by paying a deposit of £100 followed by 12 installments of £50.

Calculate the total price of the television. — 2

3. John is thinking about the future and decides to purchase life insurance.

He sees an advert in the newspaper:

Burley & Tair

Life Insurance

Monthly Premiums for every £1000 insured.

Age Male	Age Female	Non-Smoker	Smoker
16–24	16–31	£2·00	£3·00
25	32	£2·10	£3·10
26	33	£2·20	£3·20
27	34	£2·30	£3·30
28	35	£2·40	£3·40
29	36	£2·50	£3·50
30	37	£2·60	£3·60
31	38	£2·70	£3·70

John is 25 and a non-smoker. He decides to insure his life for £70 000. Calculate his monthly premium. — 3

4. In the final round of a quiz, the following scores out of 10 were recorded from participating teams.

Score	Frequency	Round Score × frequency
5	2	10
6	3	18
7	4	28
8	5	
9	4	
10	2	
	Total = 20	Total =

By completing the frequency table above, calculate the mean score of each of the 20 competing teams.

3

5. Solve algebraically the equation

$$\frac{1}{3}x + 4 = 10$$

3

6. Anne is having a new garage built.
The builder assures her that it will be completed in seven days.
The cost of materials is £1500
The builder charges £120 per day for labour.
How much should Anne have to pay in **total** for her new garage?

2

7. Work out the answers to the following.

   (a) $4 \times (-2) \times 6$

   (b) $-4 - (-10)$

8. In 1996, Africa paid an incredible $2 \cdot 3 \times 10^9$ pounds (£) in interest and debt repayments. Write this number out in full.

9. Allan wants to buy some modifications for his new car. He sees the following advert in an on-line shop:

   Mickey's Mods

Rear Lights	Chrome Exhaust	Rear Spoiler
£135	£155	£145
Front Spotlights	17" Alloy Wheels	Induction Kit
£150	£165	£130

   Allan wants to
   - buy **four** different modifications
   - stick to a strict budget of **£580**.

The table below shows **one** possible combination of 4 modifications that Allan can buy.

Rear Lights	£135					
Front Spotlights	£150					
Chrome Exhaust	£155					
17" Alloy Wheels						
Rear Spoiler						
Induction Kit	£130					
Total	£570					

Complete the above table to show all combinations of accessories that Allan can afford to buy.

3

10. The cuboid below has a volume of 420cm³.

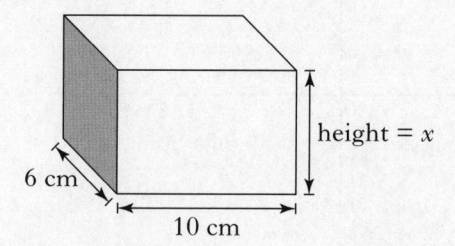

From the information above, calculate the height, x of the cuboid.

3

11. (*a*) Complete the table for $y = 0.5x - 2$.

x	−6	−2	0	8
y		−3		

(*b*) Draw the line $y = 0.5x - 2$ on the diagram below.

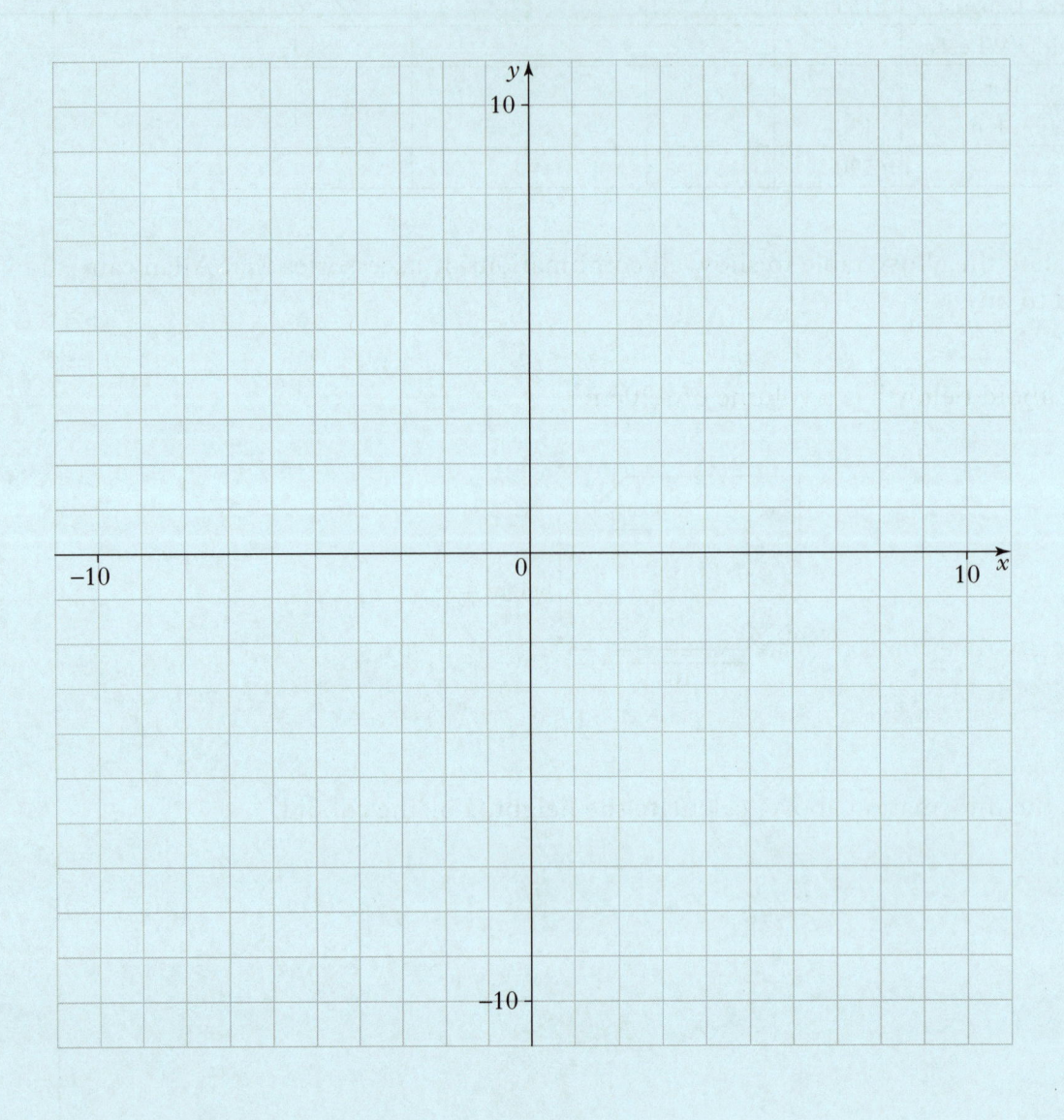

[End of Question Paper]

Mathematics | Intermediate 1 | Units 1, 2 and 3

Practice Papers
For SQA Exams

Exam D
Intermediate 1
Units 1, 2 and 3
Paper 2

You are allowed 55 minutes to complete this paper.

A calculator can be used.

Try to answer all of the questions in the time allowed, including all of your working.

Full marks will only be awarded where your answer includes any relevant working.

Practice Paper D: Intermediate 1 Mathematics Units 1, 2 and 3

Marks

1. The price of a fish supper in pounds (£) was recorded at 10 shops in a town centre:-

   3·30, 3·00, 3·50, 3·60, 3·10, 3·90, 4·20, 3·35, 4·05, 3·80

Calculate:

   (a) The mean.   2

   (b) The range.   2

   (c) Illustrate these prices in a stem-and-leaf diagram.   3

2. (a) Plot the points K(4, 4), L(–5, 1) and M(–4, –4) on the coordinate diagram below:-   2

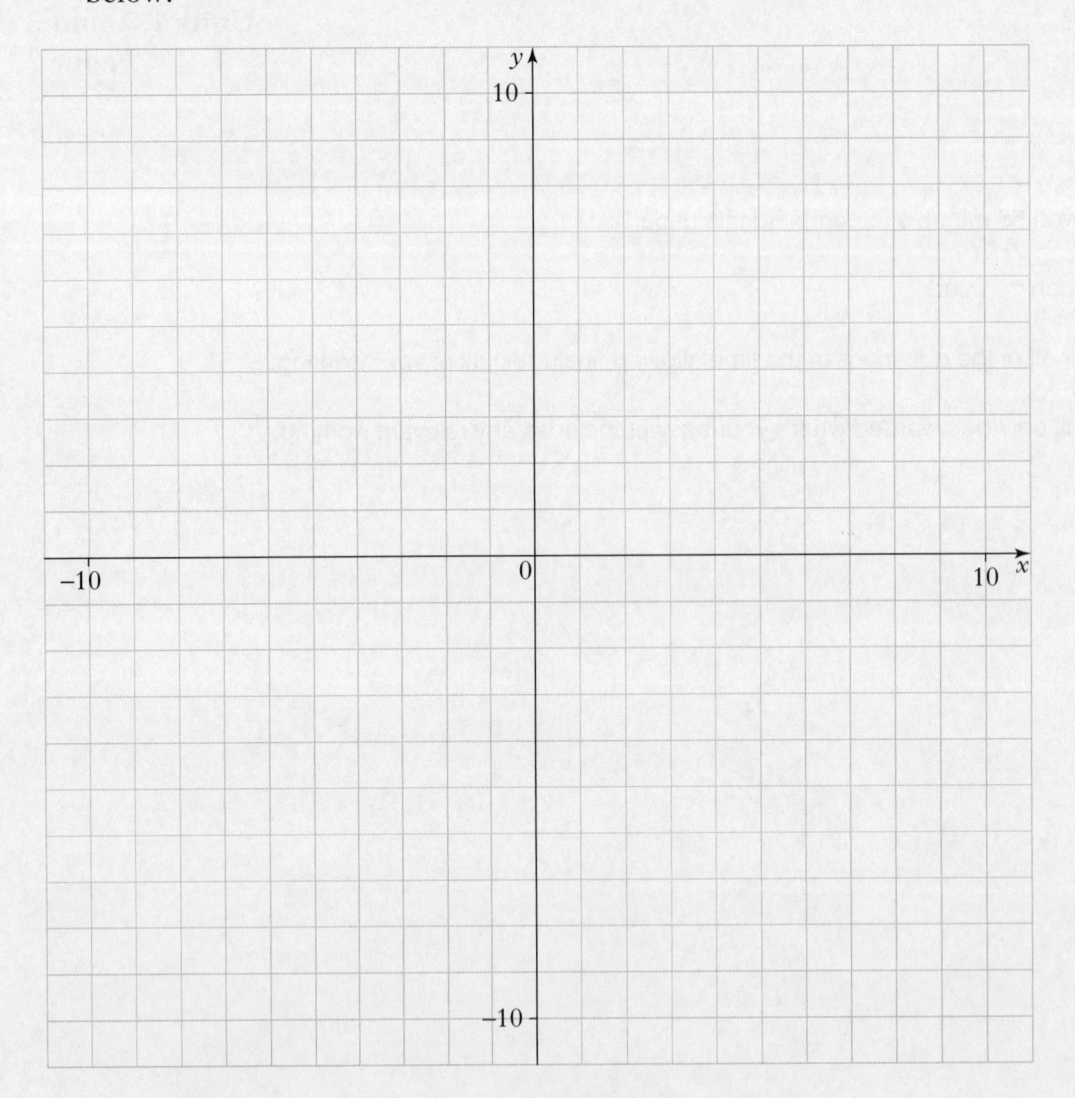

   (b) KLMN is a kite. Find the coordinates of N.   1

3. The Grand National is a famous horse race held at Aintree near Liverpool.
   A horse ran the 7¼ km distance in 12 minutes (0·2 hours).
   Calculate the horse's average speed, in **kilometres per hour**.   3

4. (a) Multiply out the brackets and simplify:

$$6x + 3(4x - 2)$$

(b) Factorise fully.

$$12x + 32$$

5. David flew from Los Angeles to Manchester for a short break taking with him 400 dollars. He spent £100 over the weekend before changing the rest into euros and flying to Milan. How many euros did David bring to Milan?
£1 = 1·60 dollars
£1 = 1·17 euros

6. Henry is on an archaeological dig. His metal detector informs him that he is 60 m away and at an angle of 20° from a metallic object buried in the ground. How far down will he have to dig?

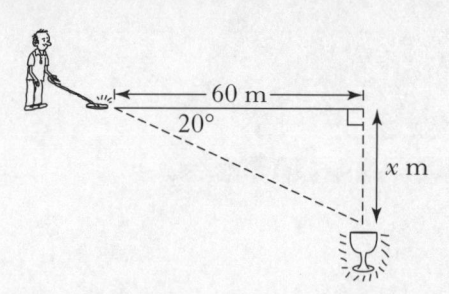

7. A motoring magazine conducted an investigation into the connection between the age of a car and its value. The results are shown in the scattergraph below:

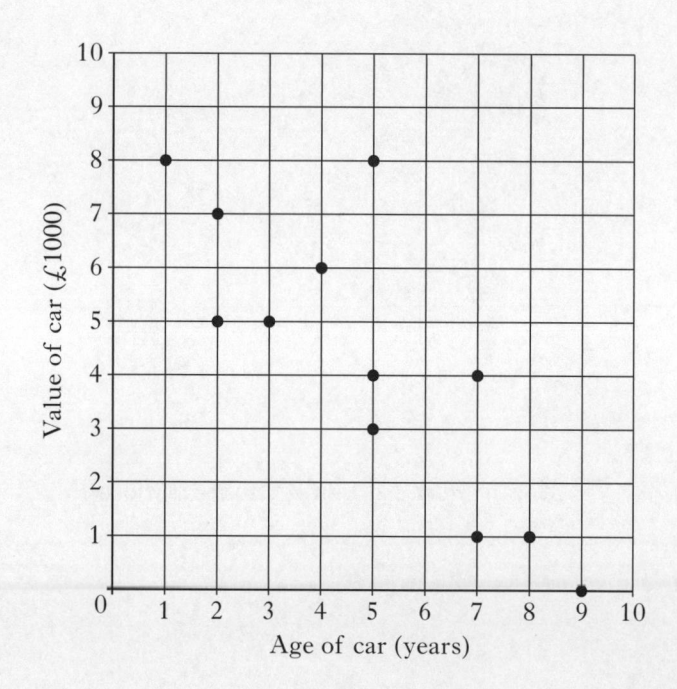

(a) On this scattergraph, draw a line of best fit.

(b) Use your line of best fit to estimate the value of a car aged 6 years.

8. Solve algebraically the inequality:

   $5x - 5 \leq 0$

   [2]

9. Lisa had an extra ticket to a rock concert which she bought for £50. With her friend unable to go she sold the ticket to her brother for £40. Calculate her loss giving your answer as a percentage of the purchase price.

   [3]

10. To warn motorists of roadworks, the council decides to put up a sign on the motorway. The sign is in the shape of an isosceles triangle with a base of 56 cm and a sloping side of 53 cm. Calculate the height of the triangle.

    [4]

11. This cardboard cut-out of a microphone is used to advertise a 'battle of the bands'. It consists of a semi-circle on top of an isosceles triangle.
    Calculate the amount of cardboard required to make the sign.

    [6]

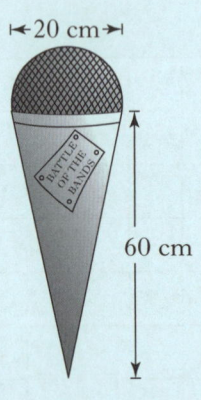

    ⟵20 cm⟶

    60 cm

12. Find the value of K when $l = 50$ and $m = 2·5$ using the formula below:

    $K = \dfrac{1}{2}l - 4m^2$

    [3]

[End of Question Paper]

Worked Answers

WORKED ANSWERS: EXAM A — PAPER 1

1.

> The non-calculator paper normally begins with some straightforward mental calculations. Use this as an opportunity to settle yourself down – and try not to make any careless mistakes!

(a) $= 6 \times 2 + 7$
  $= 12 + 7$
  $= 19$ (1)

(b) 18×3000

  $\begin{array}{r} 18 \\ \times 3 \\ \hline 54 \end{array}$ so $18 \times 3000 = 54000$ (1)

> **HINT** You must do the bracket first followed by the multiplication and the addition at the end.

(c) $1 \cdot 94$ (1)

(d) $10\% = £6$
  $20\% = 2 \times £6 = £12$ (1)

> **HINT** Be sure to line-up the decimal points.

2.

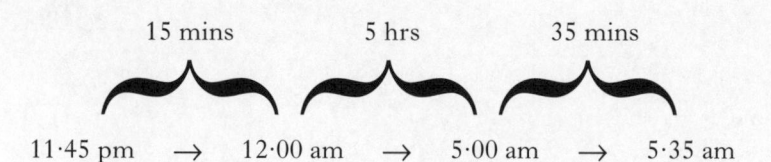

15 mins   5 hrs   35 mins

11·45 pm → 12·00 am → 5·00 am → 5·35 am

So journey time = 5 hours 50 minutes (1)

> **HINT** Using a 'counting' on method like the one shown above is a popular way to calculate time intervals.

3.

> Combination questions occur frequently in the exam and you should be systematic in your approach.

Solutions to Practice Paper A: Intermediate 1 Mathmatics Units 1, 2 and 3

Control pad		14·00	14·00	14·00	14·00			
Eye –cam	13·50	13·50		13·50		13·50		13·50
Steering wheel	14·50		14·50			14·50	14·50	
Renate control	12·00	12·00			12·00		12·00	12·00
Pro-player	15·00	15·00	15·00	15·00	15·00	15·00	15·00	15·00
Memory card			9·50	9·50	9·50	9·50	9·50	9·50
Total	55·00	54·50	53·00	52·00	50·50	52·50	51·00	50·00

> Graham *must* buy pro player so tide this box in every column first, (remember, this, only leaves him £40 to spend on 3 more items)

There are six possible answers to choose.

You receive:

1 mark for 4 correct answers
2 marks for 5 correct answers
3 marks for 6 correct answers.

HINT Remember not to spend more then £55!

4. (a) Number of goals × frequency

$$\begin{array}{r} 0 \\ 8 \\ 28 \\ 27 \\ 4 \\ 5 \end{array}\Bigg\}$$ (1)

Total = $\overline{72}$ (1)

Mean = $\dfrac{72}{36}$ = 2 goals per game (1)

HINT To get the mean from this frequency table, simply divide the total in the 'goals x frequency' column by the total in the 'frequency' column.

(b) As you can see from the table, the team scored 2 goals 14 times. This has the highest frequency. So the mode is 2. (1)

HINT The mode is the score with the highest frequency.

Solutions to Practice Paper A: Intermediate 1 Mathmatics Units 1, 2 and 3

5.

> ★ Money problems often come up in this exam.
> Always check that your answers to practical problems are practical and sensible answers.

First of all, subtract the deposit:

$$\begin{array}{r} 635 \\ -85 \\ \hline 550 \end{array}$$ (1)

This leaves a balance of £550 to be paid *evenly* over 11 months. This means we must *divide* £550 by 11.

£550 ÷ 11 = £50 (2)

6.

> ★ Scientific Notation is a way of writing really big or really small numbers quickly.

2·836 (1)
× 10^8 (1)
2·836 × 10^8

> HINT
> • The number at the start must be between 1 and 10.
> • The power is the number of times you move the decimal point.

7.

> ★ Equations appear in these exams almost every year. The 'change side, change sign' method is a popular way of solving them.

⇒ 36 − 15 = 9x − 2x (1)
⇒ 21 = 7x (1)
⇒ x = 3 (1)

> HINT
> Getting all the letters on one side and all the numbers on the other is a good place to start.

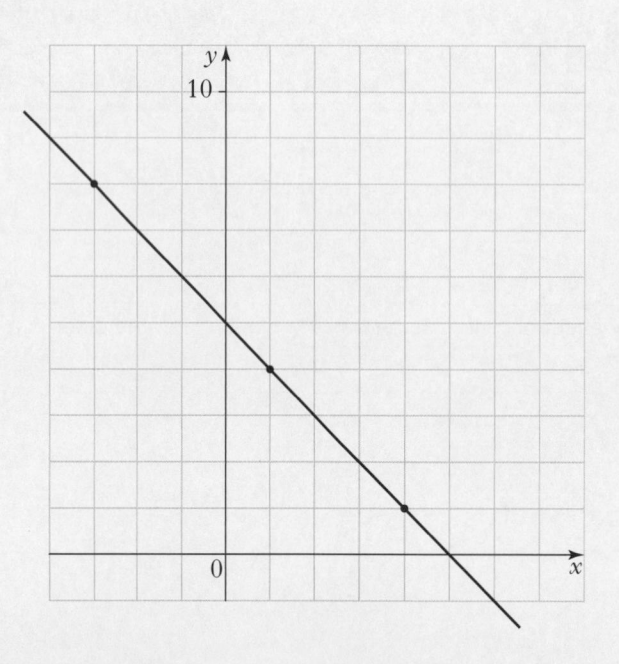

Solutions to Practice Paper A: Intermediate 1 Mathmatics Units 1, 2 and 3

8.

> Foreign exchange questions should be of use to you as this knowledge could help save you money when you go on holiday.

(a) Euros = 1·2 × 80   (1)
     = 96 €   (1)

(b) € 44 ÷ 1·2 = £36·67   (which is less than the £40 that the pupil got)   (1)

So yes, the exchange rate has changed – and for the better.   (1)

> **HINT**
> Remember, a Yes/No answer on its own will result in no marks. You must show your working!
>
> When the exchange rate to convert pounds into euros is given:
> - To change £s into €s : *multiply* by the exchange rate.
> - To change €s back into £s : *divide* by the exchange rate.

9.

> You will often be asked to draw a graph – make sure you use a pencil and a ruler.

(a)

x	−3	1	4
$y = 5-x$	8	4	1

(1)   (1)

↑ subtracting a negative, an A/B skill.

(b)

Page 56

Solutions to Practice Paper A: Intermediate 1 Mathmatics Units 1, 2 and 3

For correctly plotting *all* points. (1)

For drawing a neat straight line through the points. (1)

> **HINT** The line is supposed to go on forever, so make sure you draw it beyond the edges of the grid.

10. $\dfrac{12(2)^2}{6\times(-4)}$ For correct substitution. (1)

$= \dfrac{48}{-24}$ For tidy up. (1)

$= -2$ For correct answer. (1)

> **HINT** Remember the order in which you do things. Always square the terms before multiplying.

WORKED ANSWERS: EXAM A — PAPER 2

1.

> ★ Sometimes you will be asked to plot coordinates on a cartesian diagram – remember to go along first, then up or down.

(a)

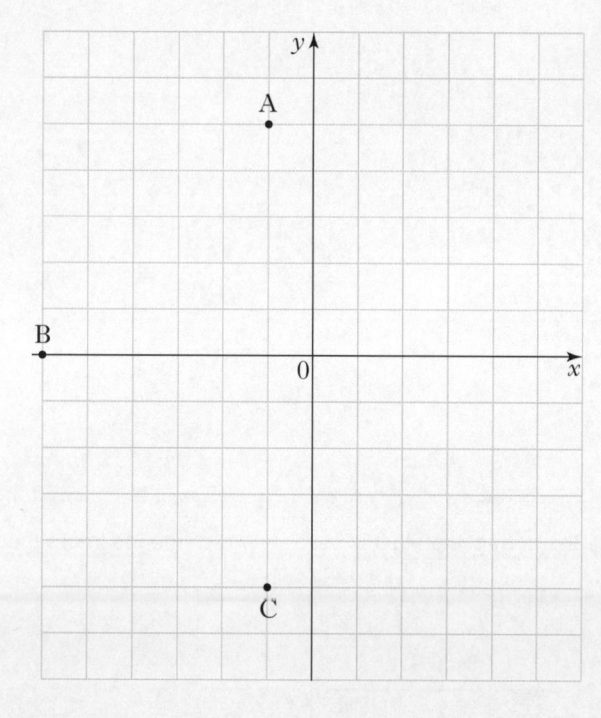

For two correct points. (1)

The third point correct. (1)

Page 57

Solutions to Practice Paper A: Intermediate 1 Mathmatics Units 1, 2 and 3

(b) For correctly plotting D (4, 0). (1)

> HINT: Remember, a square must have sides the same length.

2.

> Percentage questions come up a lot – remember, percent means 'out of 100'.

$30 - 6 = 24$ right footed players. (1)

$\dfrac{24}{30}$ (1)

$\dfrac{24}{30} \times 100 = 80\%$ (1)

3.

> Speed, distance, time problems are so much easier if you remember this triangle.

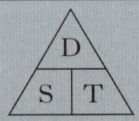

Distance = $5 \times 60 = 300$ km (1)

Time = $2\dfrac{1}{2}$ hours = 2·5 hours (1)

$S = \dfrac{D}{T}$

$= \dfrac{300}{2·5}$ (1)

= 120 kilometers per hour (1)

4. $3x > 12$ (1)
       $x > 4$ (1)

> HINT: Remember to use the correct sign in this case '>' which means 'more then'.

5.

> Pythagoras' Theorem is used to find the missing side in a right-angled triangle if there is no angle information other than that one of the angles is a right angle.

Page 58

Solutions to Practice Paper A: Intermediate 1 Mathmatics Units 1, 2 and 3

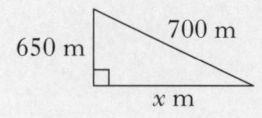

$x^2 = 700^2 - 650^2$ Take away for shorter side. (1)

$x^2 = 490000 - 422500$

$x^2 = 67500$ (1)

$x = \sqrt{67500} = 259 \cdot 8$ m (1)

HINT If you can't remember how to start these types of problems, go to the formula sheet at the start of the exam for help.

6.

★ These are three types of average – mean, median and mode. Make sure you know how to calculate each one!

(a) The data is already in order. There are two bits of data in the middle, 230 and 260.
$(260 + 230) \div 2 = 245$ the median is £245 (2)

(b) The range is $400 - 120 = £280$ (2)

(c) The median of the second site is lower. (1)
The bigger range would suggest their quotes are more variable. (1)

HINT Remember:
Volume of cuboid = length × breadth × height and 1 cm = 10 mm

7. (a) $15 \times +50$ (2)
   (b) $5(7 \times -2)$ (2)

8. $V = 60 \times 60 \times 50$ (3)
   $= 180\,000$ cm³

9. 6 cost 58·80
   1 costs $58 \cdot 80 \div 6 = £9 \cdot 80$
   7 cost $58 \cdot 80 \div 6 \times 7 = £68 \cdot 60$. (3)

10. $P = 2r^2 - 25q$

    $= 2(8)^2 - 25 \times 3 \cdot 2$ For substitution. (1)

    $= 128 - 80$ For tidy up. (1)

    $= 48$ For correct answer. (1)

HINT Although one can do the whole thing on a calculator, an isolated response of 48 is unlikely to attract any marks.

Page 59

Solutions to Practice Paper A: Intermediate 1 Mathmatics Units 1, 2 and 3

11. (a)

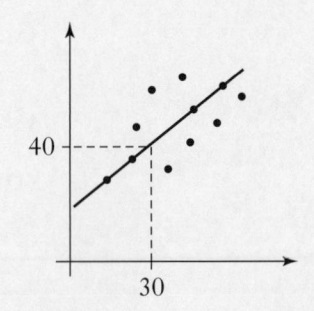

Draw a dotted line like the one above to help you. (1)

(b) 40 (1)

HINT A line of best fit should:
- follow the trend of the set of points
- roughly split the set of points into two equal groups.

12. The area of the frame can be calculated by taking the area of the smaller frame away from the larger one.

Large area = 89 × 65 = 5785 cm² (1)

Smaller area = 77 × 53 = 4081 cm² (2)

Frame = 5785 − 4081 = 1704 cm² (1)

HINT For a rectangle:
Area = length × breadth.

Page 60

13.

> If you have a problem involving a right – angled triangle along with another angle, use trigonometry.

(Hyp) 2 m, x m (opp), 6°

Decide to use 'sin' ratio. (1)

$$\sin 6° = \frac{x}{2}$$ (1)

$$x = 2 \times \sin 6° = 0 \cdot 209\ldots$$ (1)

$$= 20 \cdot 9 \text{ cm}$$ (1)

Yes, a hand rail will be required because $20 \cdot 9 > 20$ (1)

HINT Use the trigonometric ratios in the formula sheet at the front to help you.

WORKED ANSWERS: EXAM B   **PAPER 1**

1.

> ★ Make sure you thoroughly know your tables – it will make paper 1 a lot easier!

(a) 8.46
    -3.80
    $\overline{4.66}$ (1)

> HINT Remember to line up the decimal points.

(b) $\frac{2}{3}$ of $2700 = 2700 \div 3 \times 2 = 1800$ (1)

> HINT Remember, $66\frac{2}{3}\% = \frac{2}{3}$

(c) 5.6
    $\times 4$
    $\overline{22.4}$ $22.4 \times 100 = 2240$ (1)

> HINT To multiply by 400, multiply by 4, then by 100.

2. Put 6 into the number machine

$6 \to \times 12 \to +25 \to 97$

$6 \times 12 = 72$ (1)

$72 + 25 = £97$ (1)

3. $90 + 15 + 30 = 135$ mins $= 2$ hrs 15 mins (1)

$7.45 + 2$ hrs 15 mins $= 10.00$ pm (1)

Solutions to Practice Paper B: Intermediate 1 Mathmatics Units 1, 2 and 3

4.

> ★ Probability is the chance or likelihood of an event happening.

(a) $\dfrac{1}{30}$ (1)

(b) $\dfrac{3}{30}$ (1)

$= \dfrac{1}{10}$ (1)

> **HINT** A fraction should *always* be left in its simplest form.

5. $24 + 4 = 10x - 6x$ (1)

$28 = 4x$ (1)

$x = 7$ (1)

> **HINT** The 'change side, change sign' method is a good choice here.

6 (a) Number of runs × frequency

$$\left.\begin{array}{r}24\\75\\60\\49\\16\end{array}\right\}$$ (1)

Total 224 (1)

Mean = 224/40 = 5.6 (1)

(b) The mode is the number that appears most often.
5 runs are scored 15 times. This has the highest frequency. Mode = 5 runs (1)

7. £1·20 per miles means that for 7 miles it will cost 7 × £1·20.

$$\begin{array}{r}£1\cdot20\\ \times\ 7\\ \hline 8\cdot40\end{array}$$ (1)

Don't forget to add on the £3 for the hire of the taxi! £8·40 + £3·00 = £11·40 (1)

8. (a)

x	−4	0	2
$y = 4 - 2x$	12	4	0

(1) (1)

Subtracting a negative, is an A/B skill.

Page 63

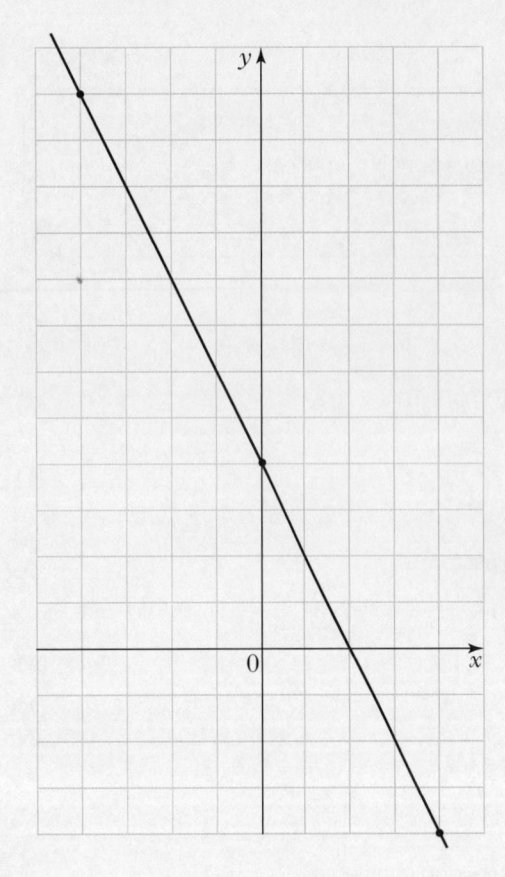

Solutions to Practice Paper B: Intermediate 1 Mathmatics Units 1, 2 and 3

(b)

(2)

> **HINT** The line is supposed to go on forever, so make sure you draw it beyond the edges of the grid.

9. $\dfrac{3ab}{c}$

$= \dfrac{3 \times (-2) \times (-5)}{9}$ For correct substitution.   **(1)**

$= \dfrac{30}{9}$ For tidy – up.   **(1)**

$= \dfrac{10}{3}$ For simplified answer.   **(1)**

> **HINT** Remember, when you multiply two negatives together, your answer will be *positive*.

10.   10% = £16

  5% = £8   **(1)**

  9 months = $\dfrac{3}{4}$ of a year   **(1)**

  $\dfrac{3}{4}$ of £8 = £6   **(1)**

Total in account after 9 months.

  = £160 + £6 = £166   **(1)**

Page 64

Solutions to Practice Paper B: Intermediate 1 Mathmatics Units 1, 2 and 3

11. $1·5 \times 10^{-1}$ For 1·5. (1)
                    For $\times 10^{-1}$. (1)

> **HINT** Very small numbers have negative powers.

WORKED ANSWERS: EXAM B   PAPER 2

1. Volume = l × b × h
   = 27 × 27 × 27 (1)
   = 19 683 cm³
   = 20 000 cm³ (to nearest thousand) (1)

2. 468 ÷ 10·40 (1)
   = £45 (1)

> **HINT** To go from kroners back to pounds, simply divide by the exchange rate.

3. (a) Put the numbers in order first!

   £690, £750, (£780), £830, £940 (1)

   Median = £780 (1)

   (b) Range = £940 − £690 = 250 (1)

> **HINT** Median = middle number
> Range = highest to lowest

   (c) The median of the high street shop is lower. (1)

   The smaller range would suggest their prices are less variable. (1)

4.

   For halfing the 6 to get 3 (1)

   $h^2 = 4^2 - 3^2$ (1)

   $h^2 = 16 - 9 = 7$ (1)

   $h = \sqrt{7} = 2.65$m (1)

(Triangle sketch: right-angled with sides h m, 4 m hypotenuse, 3 m base)

> **HINT** Sometimes it helps to make a rough sketch of the right-angled Triangle you are using.

5. $7x < 28$ (1)
   $x < 4$ (1)

Page 65

Solutions to Practice Paper B: Intermediate 1 Mathmatics Units 1, 2 and 3

> **HINT**: You can solve an inequality in a similar way to solving an equation – remember to use the correct symbol!

6. $\frac{90}{150} \times 100 = 60\%$ Correct fraction (1)

    Multiplying by 100 (1)

    Correct answer (1)

7. (a) $T = \frac{D}{S} = \frac{150}{60}$ (1)

    $= 2 \cdot 5$ hours (1)

    $= 2$ hours and 30 minutes (1)

    (b) $9 \cdot 50$ am $+ 2$ hrs 30 min $= 12 \cdot 20$ pm (1)

8. $C = 2\pi r$

    $C = 2 \times 3 \cdot 14 \times 14$

    $= 87 \cdot 92$ (4)

> **HINT**: Remember!
> $0 \cdot 5$ hrs $= 30$ minutes
> $0 \cdot 25$ hrs $= 15$ minutes
> $0 \cdot 75$ hrs $= 45$ minutes

9. (a) $7 + 40x - 10$ For expanding brackets. (1)

    $40x - 3$ For simplifying answer. (1)

> **HINT**: You must do the bracket before the addition.

    (b) $18x + 36$ For $18(\ldots)$ (1)

    $= 18(x + 2)$ For $(x + 2)$ (1)

> **HINT**: You could also put 2, 3, 6 or 9 outside the bracket but to obtain any marks you must choose the HIGHEST common factor.

10. The angle that represents tyres is

    $360 - 72 - 56 - 136 = 96°$ (1)

    $\frac{96}{360} \times 180 = 48$ cars (1)

    (1)

Solutions to Practice Paper B: Intermediate 1 Mathmatics Units 1, 2 and 3

11. $d = \sqrt{7^2 + 24^2}$ For substitution.   (1)

$\sqrt{49 + 576}$ For processing numbers.   (1)

$= \sqrt{625}$

$= 25$ units   For the answer.   (1)

12.

Area of rectangle

$= 40 \times 60 = 2400$ cm²   (1)

Radius of semi – circle

$= (60 - 20) \div 2 = 20$ cm   (1)

Area of circle

$= \pi r^2 = \pi \times 20 \times 20 = 1256$ cm²   (2)

Area of semi-circle

$= 1256 \div 2 = 628$ cm²   (1)

Area of mirror $= 2400 + 628 = 3028$ cm²   (1)

HINT The formula for the area of a circle
$A = \pi r^2$
is on the formula sheet at the beginning of the exam.

13.

Choose sin ratio   (1)

$\sin x = \dfrac{2 \cdot 5}{5}$ (1)

$x = \sin^{-1}\left(\dfrac{2 \cdot 5}{5}\right)$ (1)

$x = 30°$ (1)

HINT sin⁻¹( ) can be obtained on the calculator by pressing [shift] then [sin], although some calculators call the shift button the 2nd function. It is usually found at the top left of your calculator buttons.

Page 67

WORKED ANSWERS: EXAM C   PAPER 1

1. (a) $\begin{array}{r} 9\cdot620 \\ -3\cdot983 \\ \hline 5\cdot637 \end{array}$ (1)

> **HINT** Line up the decimal points and make use of trailing zeros where required.

(b) 5% of £70

10% = £7 (÷ 10) (1)

5% = £3·50 (÷ 2) (1)

> **HINT** You could divide by 20 instead because 5% = $\frac{1}{20}$.

(c) $\frac{5}{9}$ of 135 $\begin{array}{r} 15 \\ \times 5 \\ \hline 75 \end{array}$ (1)

$9\frac{15}{135}$ (1)

2. 07·10 + 3 hours 20 minutes = 10·30 (1)

Don't forget to add on an extra hour!

11·30 (or 11·30 am) (1)

3. To insure a flat for £1000 it will cost £2·50

To insure a flat for £80,000 it will cost

80 × £2·50 (1)

= £200 (1)

4. $1\cdot344 \times 10^6$

1·344 (1)

$\times 10^6$ (1)

68

Solutions to Practice Paper C: Intermediate 1 Mathmatics Units 1, 2 and 3

5.

Coffee Table	£25	£25	£25	£25	25
Side Table	£15	£15		£15	
Shelving Unit					40
Set of Cushions	£10	£10	£10		10
Rug	£20		£20	£20	20
Lamp		£30	£30	£30	
Total	£70	£80	£85	£90	95

Stewart *must* buy a coffee table so take this box in every column first. (remember this only leaves him £75 to spend on 3 more items.

There are 5 possible answers to choose.

You receive:

1 Mark – for 3 correct answers.
2 Marks – for 4 correct.
3 Marks – for 5.

HINT Remember not to spend more than £100!

6. (a) $3 \times (-3) \times 3 = (-9) \times 3 = -27$ (1)

(b) $12 - (-8) = 12 + 8 = 20$ (1)

HINT Remember, a double negative makes a positive.

7. To complete the table we must add a third column, the number of coins x frequency.

Number of coins	Frequency	Number of coins × Frequency
1	9	9
2	12	24
3	18	54
4	4	16
5	5	25
6	2	12
	Total = 50	Total = 140

For column. (1)

For correct entries. (1)

For total. (1)

Mean = 140 ÷ 50 = 2·8 (1)

8. $3x^2 - 2y$

$= 3(-2)^2 - 2(3)$ For correct substitution. (1)

$= 12 - 6$ For tidy – up. (1)

$= 6$ For answer. (1)

HINT Be sure to show *all* working.

Page 69

Solutions to Practice Paper C: Intermediate 1 Mathmatics Units 1, 2 and 3

9. $7x - 3 > 39$

$\Rightarrow \ 7x > 42$ (1)

$\Rightarrow \ x > 6$ (1)

> **HINT** Make sure you use the correct inequality sign!

10. (a)

x	-2	0	1
$y = 2 - 4x$	10	2	-2

(1) (1)

Subtracting one negative integer from another is an A/B skill.

(b)

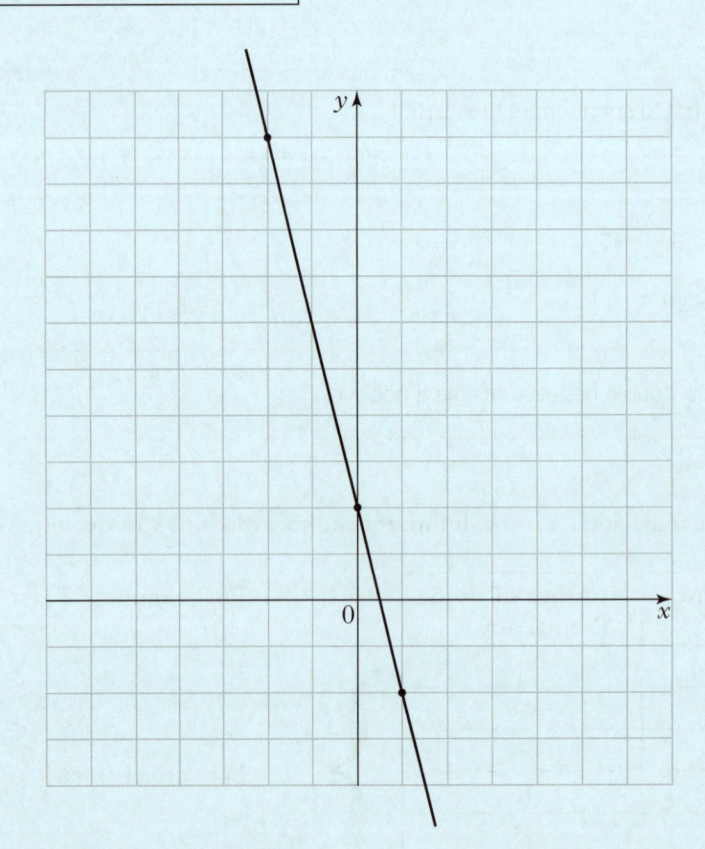

For correctly plotting **all** points. (1)

For drawing a neat straight line through the points. (1)

> **HINT** The line is infinite – make sure you draw it the full length of the grid.

Solutions to Practice Paper C: Intermediate 1 Mathmatics Units 1, 2 and 3

11. It is *not* sunny for $365 - 300 = 65$ days. (1)

$$P_{(\text{not sunny})} = \frac{65}{365}$$ (1)

$$= \frac{13}{73}$$ (1)

> **HINT** Remember, to obtain full marks a fraction must *always* be left in its simplest form.

WORKED ANSWERS: EXAM C — PAPER 2

1. (a)

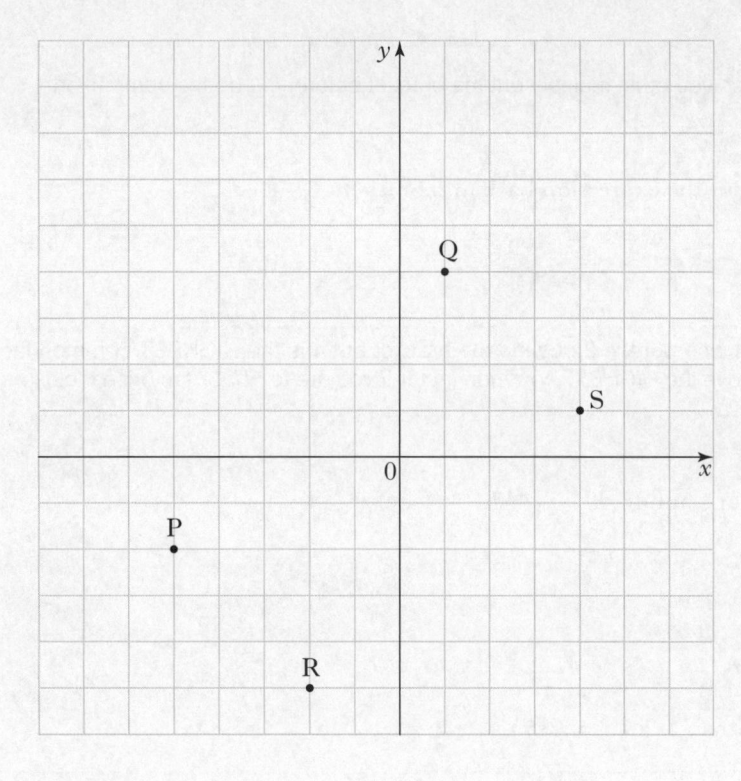

(2)

(b) For 4th point S.

For 2 correct points.

For 3rd point. (1)

> **HINT** To get from P to Q we must take 6 steps to the right and 6 steps up. To get from R to S, we must do the same.

Page 71

Solutions to Practice Paper C: Intermediate 1 Mathmatics Units 1, 2 and 3

2. (a) mean = $\dfrac{173}{10}$ (1)

   = 17·3 kg (1)

   (b) To calculate the median, remember to put the numbers in order first.

   10, 12, 14, 15, ⓘ8, ⓘ8, 19, 20, 23, 24 (1)

   In this case, there is no middle number.
   To obtain the median, simply find the mean of the two middle numbers.

   Median = $\dfrac{18+18}{2}$ = 18 (1)

3. (a) $4(3x - 2) - 5x$

   = $12x - 8 - 5x$ For multiplying out bracket. (1)

   = $7x - 8$ For tidy up. (1)

   HINT   Remember, you must multiply out the bracket before you do the subtraction.

   (b) Factorise means put the expression back into brackets.

   $16 - 12x$ For the 4 (…). (1)

   = $4(4 - 3x)$ For the $(4-3x)$. (1)

   HINT   You could also put the 2 outside the bracket but 4 is the HIGHEST common factor. You must remove the HIGHEST common factor if you are to FULLY factorise the expression.

4. Percent means 'out of one hundred.'

   $\dfrac{3}{100} \times £3500 = £105$ (1)

   4 months is $\dfrac{1}{3}$ of a year (1)

   So interest after 4 months £105 ÷ 3 = £35 (1)

   HINT   'per annum' means 'per year.'

5.

   x m, 12 m, 5 m

   $x^2 = 5^2 + 12^2$ (1)

   $x^2 = 25 + 144$

   $x^2 = 169$ (1)

   $x = \sqrt{169}$ = 13 m (1)

   HINT   If two sides of a right angled triangle are known, you can always find the third side by using Pythagoras' Theorem.

   The formula sheet may help you here.

Solutions to Practice Paper C: Intermediate 1 Mathmatics Units 1, 2 and 3

6. $13x - 2 = 6x + 19$

$\Rightarrow 13x - 6x = 19 + 2$ For 'x's' on one side, and numbers on the other. **(1)**

$7x = 21$ For tidy up. **(1)**

$x = 3$ For answer. **(1)**

7. Change the dollars ($) into pounds (£)

$\$2160 \div 1 \cdot 80 = £1200$ **(1)**

$£1200 - £800 = £400$ **(1)**

Now change the pounds (£) into euros (€).

$£400 \times 1 \cdot 17 = 468$ € **(1)**

> **HINT**: To change pounds (£) to foreign currency simply *multiply* by the exchange rate.
> To change foreign currency back into pounds (£) simply *divide* by the exchange rate.

8. Profit $= 225 - 200 = £25$ **(1)**

$\dfrac{25}{200} \times 100 = 12.5\%$ For correct fraction. **(1)**

    For answer. **(1)**

9. $A = \sqrt{b + c}$

$= \sqrt{4 \cdot 3 + 11 \cdot 7}$ For correct substitution. **(1)**

$= \sqrt{16}$ For tidy up. **(1)**

$= 4$ For correct answer. **(1)**

10.

250 m (adj), 35°, x m (opp)

For correctly naming sides. **(1)**

$\tan 35° = \dfrac{x}{250}$ **(1)**

$x = 250 \times \tan 35°$ **(1)**

$x = 175 \cdot 1$ m **(1)**

> **HINT**: The trigonometric definitions in the formula sheet may help you here.

Page 73

Solutions to Practice Paper C: Intermediate 1 Mathmatics Units 1, 2 and 3

11. Calculate the correct angle first:

    Angle = 360 − 84 − 96 − 144 = 36° (1)

    So the number of pupils who went

    to America is: For correct fraction. (1)

    $\frac{36}{360} \times 30 = 3$ pupils   For multiplying by 30. (1)

    > **HINT**   All the angles in a pie chart add up to 360°

12. The volume of a cube can be obtained by the formula:

    $v = l \times b \times h$ or $v = l^3$

    If $v = l^3$ then $l\sqrt[3]{v}$ (1)

    $= l\sqrt[3]{216}$ (1)

    $= 6$ cm (1)

    (You can check your answer $6 \times 6 \times 6 = 216$)

    > **HINT**   Make sure you know where the 'cube root' button on your calculator is.

13. For this question you will have to work out the area of each pizza slice, then state which one has the greatest area.

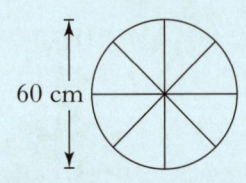

    Area of full pizza = πr^2
                         = 3·14 × 30 × 30
                         = 2826 cm² (1)

    Area of 1 slice = 2826 ÷ 8
                     = 353·25 cm² (1)

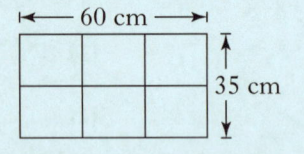

    Area of full pizza = $l \times b$
                         = 60 × 35 = 2100 cm² (1)

    Area of 1 slice = 2100 ÷ 6
                     = 350 cm² (1)

    A slice of deep pan pizza has a larger area. (1)

    > **HINT**   After all your working, make sure you answer the question!
    > The formula sheet at the start of the exam may help you here.

WORKED ANSWERS: EXAM D   PAPER 1

1. (a) 16·37
       +9·00

        25·37   (1)

   25·37
   −4·80

   20·57   (1)

> **HINT** Make use of trailing zeros where required. Be careful not to make any careless mistakes!

(b) $0·39 \times 10 = 3·9$

       3·9
       × 4

      15·6   (1)

> **HINT** To multiply a number by 40, multiply by 10 first, then by 4.

2. 12 equal installments would cost:

    50
   ×12
   ----
   600   (1)

Don't forget to add on the deposit!

Total cost = 600 + 100 = £700   (1)

3. For John to insure his life for £1000, it would cost £2·10

For interpreting the table.   (1)

For John to insure his life for £70,000 it would cost

   $70 \times £2·10$ (1)
   $= £147$ (1)

4.

Score	Frequency	Score × Frequency
5	2	10
6	3	28
7	4	28
8	5	40
9	4	36
10	2	20
	Total = 20	Total = 162

For completing column.   (1)

For correct total.   (1)

Mean = 162 ÷ 20 = 8·1   (1)

Solutions to Practice Paper D: Intermediate 1 Mathmatics Units 1, 2 and 3

5. $\frac{1}{3}x + 4 = 10$ (1)

    $\frac{1}{3}x = 6$ (1)

    $x = 18$ (1)

6. Find out the cost of labour for 7 days:

$$\begin{array}{r} 120 \\ \times\,70 \\ \hline 840 \end{array}$$ (1)

Don't forget to add on the cost of the materials!

Total = 840 + 1500 = £2340   (1)

7. (a) $4 \times (-2) \times 6 = (-8) \times 6 = -48$ (1)

    (b) $-4 - (-10) = -4 + 10 = 6$ (1)

HINT Remember, subtracting a negative integer makes a positive.

8.   2,300,000,000   (2)

9.

Rear Lights	£135	£135	£135	£135	£135	
Front Spot lights	£150	£150	£150			£150
Chrome Exhaust	£155			£155		£155
17" Alloy Wheels		£165			£165	
Rear Spoiler			£145	£145	£145	£145
Induction Kit	£130	£130	£130	£130	£130	£130
Total	£570	£580	£560	£565	£575	£580

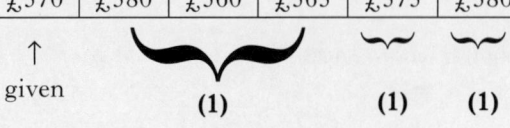

↑ given   (1)   (1)   (1)

HINT Remember not to spend more than £580!

10. $6 \times 10 = 60$ (1)

    $\frac{420}{60}$ (1)

    = 7 cm   (1)

HINT Volume = l × b × h.
If you are being asked to find either l, b or h instead of the volume, you will have to divide.

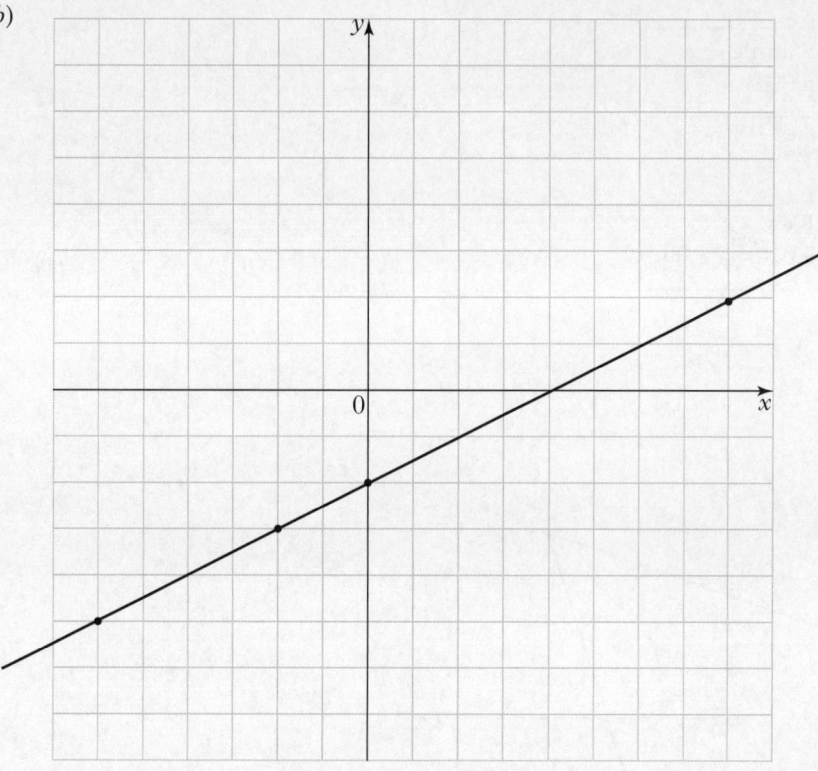

Solutions to Practice Paper D: Intermediate 1 Mathmatics Units 1, 2 and 3

11. (a)

x	−6	0	8
$y = 0·5x − 2$	−5	−2	2

For two correct points. **(1)**

For all three correct. **(1)**

(b)

For plotting all points correctly. **(1)**

For drawing a neat straight line through all the points. **(1)**

> **HINT** The line is infinite so make sure you draw it the full length of the grid.

WORKED ANSWERS: EXAM D   PAPER 2

1. (a) Mean = $\dfrac{173}{10}$ **(1)**

= 1·73 **(1)**

> **HINT** Mean = $\dfrac{\text{total of all suppers}}{\text{number of suppers}}$

(b) Range = £4·20 − £3·00 = £1·20 **(2)**

> **HINT** Range = Highest to Lowest

Page 77

Solutions to Practice Paper D: Intermediate 1 Mathmatics Units 1, 2 and 3

(c)   Cost of fish suppers

```
3·0 | 0
3·1 | 0
3·2 |
3·3 | 0 5
3·4 |
3·5 | 0
3·6 | 0
3·7 |
3·8 | 0
3·9 | 0
4·0 | 5
4·1 |
4·2 | 0
```

For *ordered* stem – and - leaf diagram.   (1)

Sample size
n = 10   (1)

Key:
3.0 | 0 = £3.00   (1)

2. (a)

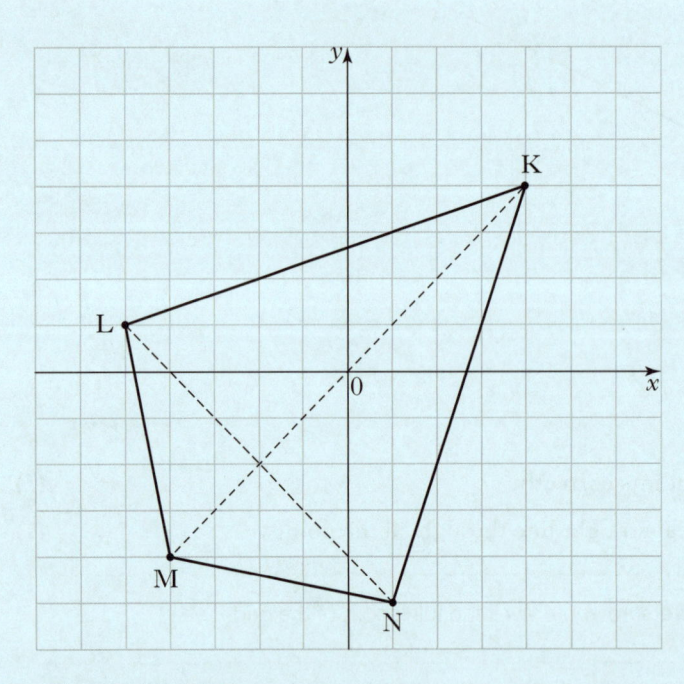

For any two points.   (1)
The third.   (1)

(b) N(1, −5)   (1)

HINT MK is a line of symmetry. N is the image of L in MK.

3. $7\frac{1}{4}$ km = 7·25 km   (1)

$S = \dfrac{D}{T} = \dfrac{7\cdot 25}{0\cdot 2}$ (1)

= 36·25 kph   (1)

HINT Remember your Triangle:-

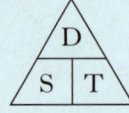

It saves you remembering the 3 different equations.

Page 78

Solutions to Practice Paper D: Intermediate 1 Mathmatics Units 1, 2 and 3

4. (a) $= 6x + 12x - 6$ (1)

$= 18x - 6$ (1)

> **HINT** You must do the *bracket* before the *subtraction*.

(b) $4(3x + 8)$ (2)

> **HINT** You could also take out '2' but '4' is the *highest common factor*. You must take out the HCF to obtain full marks.

5. $400\$ \div 1\cdot 6 = £250$ (1)

$250 - 100 = £150$ (1)

$£150 \times 1\cdot 17 = 175\cdot 5 €$ (1)

> **HINT** £s to foreign currency *multiply* by the exchange rate foreign currency to £s, *divide* by exchange rate.

6.

60 m (adj), 20°, h m (opp)

Correctly naming sides (1)

$\tan 20° = \dfrac{h}{60}$ (1)

$h = 60 \times \tan 20$ (1)

$h = 21\cdot 8$ m (1)

> **HINT** You may find the formula sheet at the front of the exam sheet helpful here.

7. (a) (1)

Draw a dotted line like the one above to help you.

(b) £3000 (1)

Page 79

Solutions to Practice Paper D: Intermediate 1 Mathmatics Units 1, 2 and 3

8. $5x - 5 \leq 0$

$5x \leq 5$ (1)

$x \leq 1$ (1)

> **HINT** Make sure you use the correct inequality symbol!

9. $\dfrac{10}{50} \times 100 = 20\%$

For loss of $50 - 40 = £10$ (1)

For correct fraction. (1)

For correct answer. (1)

10. By drawing a line down the middle of the road sign, we can split it into 2 right-angled triangles.

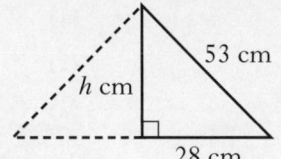

For halving 56 to get 28. (1)

$h^2 = 53^2 - 28^2$ (1)

$h^2 = 2025$ (1)

$h = \sqrt{2025} = 45$ cm (1)

> **HINT** If you are asked to find the missing side of a right-angled triangle when you know the other 2, you can use Pythagoras' Theorem.

11.

> ★ It can help to split problems like these into separate shapes.

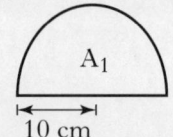

$A_1 = \pi r^2 \div 2$ (1)

$= 3 \cdot 14 \times 10 \times 10 \div 2$ (1)

$= 157$ cm^2 (1)

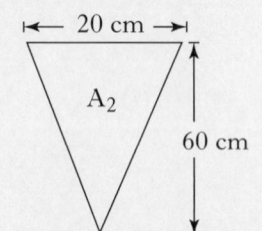

$A_2 = \dfrac{1}{2} \times 20 \times 60$ (1)

$= 600$ cm^2 (1)

Total area $= 157 + 600 = 757$ cm^2 (1)

> **HINT** The formula sheet at the front of the exam contains vital formulae should you forget them on the day of the exam!

12. $K = \dfrac{1}{2} 1 - 4 m^2$

$K = \dfrac{1}{2}(50) - 4(2 \cdot 5)^2$ For correct substitution. (1)

$= 25 - 25$ For tidy-up. (1)

$= 0$ For answer. (1)

Page 80